GET OFF

THE
BENCH

SIDNEY E. FUCHS

GET OFF THE BENCH

UNLEASHING THE POWER OF STRATEGIC NETWORKING THROUGH RELATIONSHIPS

Advantage®

Published by Advantage, Charleston, South Carolina.
Member of Advantage Media Group.

ADVANTAGE is a registered trademark and the Advantage colophon is a trademark of Advantage Media Group, Inc.

Printed in the United States of America.

ISBN: 978-1-59932-256-8
LCCN: 2012936716

This publication is designed to provide accurate and authoritative information in regard to the subject matter covered. It is sold with the understanding that the publisher is not engaged in rendering legal, accounting, or other professional services. If legal advice or other expert assistance is required, the services of a competent professional person should be sought.

Advantage Media Group is proud to be a part of the Tree Neutral® program. Tree Neutral offsets the number of trees consumed in the production and printing of this book by taking proactive steps such as planting trees in direct proportion to the number of trees used to print books. To learn more about Tree Neutral, please visit www.treeneutral.com. To learn more about Advantage's commitment to being a responsible steward of the environment, please visit www.advantagefamily.com/green

Advantage Media Group is a leading publisher of business, motivation, and self-help authors. Do you have a manuscript or book idea that you would like to have considered for publication? Please visit www.amgbook.com or call 1.866.775.1696

DEDICATION

The author wishes to dedicate this book to his family—Susan, Bill, Bobby, and Jim. Without their love, support, and patience, my life's journey, and this book, would not have been possible. The author also wants to thank his parents, Bill and Yvonne, for teaching him the value of people, how to help others, and what it means to get off the bench.

ACKNOWLEDGEMENTS

The author wishes to thank the following people for their support, guidance, and valuable feedback during this process: Susan Fuchs, Dr. Lois Frankel, Steve Mann, PaShon Mann, Tom Finn, Scott Eblin, JD Kathuria, Brian Kumnick, and Bill Weber. Their time and effort spent on helping me work through this book is very much appreciated and can never be repaid.

Where would we be without mentors? I've been fortunate in my life to have some of the best – Dr. Robert Courter, Dennis Adams, Walker Royce, General Rich O'Lear, Dr. John Lehman, Tig Krekel, General Peter Schoomaker, Admiral Ann Rondeau, General Michael Dunn, Renny DiPentima, Peter Marino, Jim Frey, Evans Hineman and many others.

The following are actual texts and emails sent to the author, Sid Fuchs, that demonstrate the power of the network:

ONE:

Sid, thanks for reminding me about the Tower Club networking event on Monday. I got an interview with XYZ bank out of it...

TWO:

Friends:

If you are receiving this, you are one of the many, many good friends and colleagues that have met with, advised, introduced, encouraged, challenged, and otherwise helped me over the last 4 months as I have charted the course for my next professional role. I cannot say enough about that process—I got to reconnect with a lot of great folks and meet some fantastic new friends along the way, and I learned far more than I ever imagined I could have.

Perhaps the greatest lesson that was affirmed for me during this time is that the contacts and relationships we have are best used when freely shared, regardless of a calculated benefit any of us might be able to project beforehand. Many of you did that for me along the way, and the meetings and introductions that came about as a result were invaluable. The truth is you simply do not know what great things you might be putting into motion when you introduce two people in the marketplace.

Now here's the update—I am happy to report that I have accepted an offer to serve as President & COO of XYZ Associates, a portfolio company of The ABC Group, and will be starting at the end of this month. XYZ is a government services firm operating in the national security arena, mainly with State Department and

Homeland Security. Life in the days ahead will be about maturing and integrating several business segments that currently make up roughly $XXXM in revenues, with significant opportunity to grow that organically and through acquisition. I am quite confident that we both took the requisite time to get to know each other over the last several months, so this is a great fit that I am extremely excited about.

I look forward to staying in touch with all of you. I think it goes without saying—given the message above—that if there is ANYTHING I might do for you, to include making an introduction to a friend or colleague on your behalf, I would be honored to help in any way I can.

THREE:
AS A FOLLOW ON TO THE PREVIOUS EMAIL ABOVE:

Thank you, Sid. Just so you know—you can take great credit for me finding this particular role. After you and I spoke, your conversation with the guys at the BBB Group led them to speak to Joe Smith at ABC, who had just bought XYZ…and there you have it.

I really appreciate your willingness to do that for me—and I'm happy to repay the favor in kind. I owe you one—at least—down the line. Would be my pleasure to help you out in any way I can sometime soon.

Four:
And a final email from the same person when I asked him for details on how the network helped him during his job search:

When we knew that a transaction was imminent and I decided that I was going to go another route—I called or emailed 7 people to get some thoughts and perspective on what to do next. That's it. Those 7 turned into 247 face-to-face meetings over the next 6 months... mostly with people that I did not know or know well enough to meet with when I started the process. Just for grins, I charted it all out and it's amazing to look at. I not only used the network, I NEEDED it...

TABLE OF CONTENTS

INTRODUCTION

Julie, a thirty-eight-year-old marketing executive, was recently laid off from her marketing firm. Julie had many people depending on her: she was married and had three young children, and her job provided her family with its primary income source. It didn't help that the economy was struggling and unemployment was at an all-time high. Still, Julie had several things going for her. She was well liked in the business community and well connected to many friends. Most importantly, she had a solid reputation of honesty and integrity.

Sitting down with a friend over coffee, Julie wondered what she was going to do and how she was going to make ends meet. She was nervous and anxious, but excited at the same time. This was her chance to decide her future: should she go to work for another large firm, or strike out on her own?

As Julie went over with her friend the types of things she could do for or bring to a business, her friend started to ask her a few questions. "What are your strengths and where can you really add value?"

Julie answered that her knowledge of the industry, her breadth and depth of contacts, and her business experience were all valuable assets.

Her friend honed in on this point and said, "That may all be true, but what is the number one asset that makes you different from everyone else? What is your competitive advantage?"

Julie's response was all over the map: she couldn't focus. Finally, her friend said to her, "From where I sit, your value proposition is that you know everyone in town. You've spent the past several years coordinating and leading some of the premier marketing and networking events in town. Your network is your most valuable asset."

At that point, Julie realized that her network—the friendships and business partnerships she'd spent years developing—was of great value. That network could help someone like her, someone who needed to be connected with, promoted in, or exposed to people in the right circles. She understood that she had real relationships at almost every level of industry and government. Moreover, her network could help her when she needed that help. Julie realized that *relationships are tangible assets with real value*. They should be nurtured, protected, and invested in—you should treat them the same way you would treat anything of value.

After this realization, Julie decided to start her own marketing company. As she was starting out, she also picked up a few consulting assignments, working with small companies whose proprietors wanted to grow their businesses. The proprietors of these small companies knew that growth required a connection to larger companies—a connection that could offer partnering, mentoring, and investment opportunities. In what seemed like no time at all, Julie's new company was hosting events all over town. These events included some very big names from government and industry—people who had known Julie for years and were eager to help her. After all, *trust is the currency of all relationships* and Julie's network trusted and respected her.

Her new clients, mostly "unconnected" folks now had chances to meet with the "connected"—people who had eluded them for many years. Julie was connecting people in different networks and helping those people achieve their goals. Along the way, she helped herself, too. All of this happened because she had developed a broad network of friends and partners throughout her career.

Now, let's imagine that Julie had not developed the network described above. What would her options have been then? She would have been limited to searching job boards (along with the millions of others looking for work), reaching out to recruiters (who probably wouldn't have known her, which in itself would have put her at a disadvantage), and sending out dozens of resumes to companies. At this point, it would have been very apparent to Julie that she didn't know the right people. Then, a hard truth would have hit her right between the eyes: *When you need a relationship, it's too late to build it.*

Julie's story is just one example of the value maintaining a strategic network provides. All of the elements that will be discussed in this book came into play during Julie's journey to, and the eventual creation of, her new company. While not all the people who read this book will be on a trajectory like Julie's—that of starting their own company—the principles and techniques discussed here will certainly add to their everyday lives.

I'm a musician, Harley rider, business leader, and writer who hails from New Orleans. I have two engineering degrees, and I was an intelligence officer with the Central Intelligence Agency for many years. These are things I often work into conversation when I first meet someone because I know they are an unusual combination. Usually, people are unsure how to react to me. It makes them wonder: Is this guy Sid an easy-going, artistic type from the South? Is he someone who enjoys a good time and takes a big-picture approach to life, or is he a vigilant, analytical type who probes for details?

The left-brained, analytical side of me requires that I go through life with a plan: that part of me wants to manage outcomes constantly and to leave very little to chance. The other side of me, the one that is rooted in Algiers Point (a section of New Orleans) and my Mark Twain-style childhood, requires personal, human contact as an everyday practice. My point is, the two sides go together. I use what I learn and what I intuit from interacting casually with people to get things accomplished within organizations and groups. I have a need for accomplishment and achievement, and I have a need to relate to people and understand them. Trust me, those traits don't conflict with each other—they reinforce each other.

The human aspect of my childhood was intense and up-close. We had no choice but to get tuned in to people and interested in what made them tick. New Orleans is an extremely social place; its locals include many extended families made up of people who have stayed in the same neighborhoods for generations. In New Orleans, you never had to look far to find a reason to have a party, a social event, or a gathering. It was a way of life. You were expected to know your neighbors, schoolmates, extended family members, and friends on a personal level. Everyone knew each other's business and was there for help if you needed it. For example, the locals know that if you get a speeding ticket in New Orleans, who you know may get you out of paying the ticket. Need New Orleans Saints tickets? Call someone's uncle. Want to ride on a Mardi Gras float? Call my friend's dad. When it was time for me to leave home and enter the working world, I kept the New Orleans habit of making time for people and finding ways we could build friendships and perhaps help each other.

Over the past twenty-plus years, I have built a very broad, productive, and powerful network that has allowed me the good fortune of a fulfilling career. I have been a CEO many times over, run billion-dollar divisions for Fortune 100 companies, fulfilled three political appointments, performed charity work, served as board chairman of a premier private business club, and held many other board and advisory positions and appointments all while ensuring I made time for my personal life so I could enjoy my wonderful wife and three boys. I've been blessed in building many wonderful and long-lasting friendships, which have enhanced my life in many ways. I owe many of my accomplishments to the network I've created, and today, I continue networking just for fun.

Although networking seems like second nature to me, and since I know many people and I'm well connected, I'm amazed by how many people in industry, commerce, and the professions do not understand networking's value. This lack of recognition is the reason I wrote this book. I want you to know the same thing I tell people constantly: "It's not about how many college degrees you have, where you went to school, or how much money you make. It's about who you know." *I wrote this book to help people build and maintain a network of relationships in order to make the most of their abilities and enjoy their lives and careers to the fullest.*

For some people, this approach to life and work has to be learned. It doesn't come to them in a way that feels instinctive and innate. I'm convinced networking can be a *natural thing for all of us*, as we go about our work and go about our lives by relating to each other. I've thought about this topic for a long time, and I don't consider myself unusual in what I want or need from life. However, I am somewhat unusual in the way I act on my needs and achieve my work—life balance. If that last statement gets you thinking, that is a good thing.

I learned early on that the majority of interacting with other people is learning from them. If I met someone for the first time at a reception, picnic, or civic event and we talked for a while, someone else who knows me might say, "There's Sid; he's met a new person and he's networking." Which is fine—of all people, I don't object to the term "networking." That's the central topic of this book and it's a thread that runs through my entire life and career.

But really, in that instance, what's happening is that I'm keeping the conversation going until that new person tells me something I didn't know before. Usually, it will be a small detail about that person's life or interests. The detail could be the discovery that we know someone in common or the realization that something is happening in our region or industry. While that detail will probably seem unimportant at the time, it's important to me because it helps me understand what this new person is about, how he or she sees the world, or maybe where he or she is headed in life.

Networking is an art as much as a skill. To become competent at networking, you must invest time meeting people and working to understand each individual's personality. You only get this skill through experience. If you're not building a networking activity into your daily routine and you're not trying to understand those around you, you'll never gain that experience. As a result, you'll lack the skills, experience, and techniques required to effectively network and create strategic relationships that can help you in every facet of your life.

When I meet someone new, the question I'm thinking is: What is this person's life all about? What makes him or her happy or unhappy? So many times in first meetings—in Washington, D.C., anyway— the initial question is about where people work. The subtext for that question is to determine if people are successful professionally or are moving up the ladder. However, when I get introduced to people, I don't immediately ask them where they work because that doesn't tell me much about *who* they are.

I should say one quick thing about professional success as it relates to interpersonal relationships: If you truly have a network of trusted contacts and allies, the periods when you aren't experiencing success will be easier to get through. Despite all the success I've enjoyed, I've also had my fair share of failures and screw-ups; however, I've always learned from them and moved on. I've never beaten myself up too much. In part, that's because the people in my network—my colleagues, partners, and associates—have gone through their own share of setbacks and flops. I know all about these setbacks because the people in my network and I have enough trust to talk about them. We've been able to help each other get past the rough spots and eventually laugh about them.

Before you can really work with or lead someone, you've got to have a stake in the relationship. That can't happen unless there is a natural give and take. You have to connect with each person in a way that accommodates both of your personalities and styles. For example, when I was running a division at one large company, one of the gentlemen who worked for me was a bit older than his peers (he was more than twenty years older than I was). To be honest, he was much more grumpy, skeptical, and ornery than most of our colleagues.

However, I got to know this gentleman and learned that he was a Vietnam veteran and a candidate for the Congressional Medal of Honor; I also learned he had an incredible talent for customer development and business strategy. After that, I was impressed by and in awe of his history and talent. I knew I had to connect with him in a way that ensured mutual respect. He wouldn't do what I asked him to just because I was his boss (especially since I would have been a "kid" in his eyes). This was a guy who would charge the hill and take gunfire for you if he believed in you. He was also the type who would dog you repeatedly if he thought you were faking it or didn't deserve his respect. He tested me constantly to see how far he could push me, but I stood my ground, showed him respect, and worked to build a relationship with him so he would work with me instead of against me. After many months, he finally accepted me. To this day, almost ten years later, we are good friends and keep in touch. I know that he would do anything for me and he knows I would do the same for him. Without taking the approach of building a real relationship (which also meant letting him "drive" on occasion), and keeping my larger goal in mind (how to leverage this incredible talent for the success of our customers and our division), our interactions would have turned out very differently. If my ego had been in charge in this situation, our relationship would have ended right there and then.

Ultimately, people want to be known to each other. They want to reveal at least part of themselves. Now, they don't make these reveals with big dramatic declarations or confessions, like in bad movies. They reveal themselves in small comments and statements, which take on meaning if you're listening and putting two and two together. Pretty soon, you know these other people well enough to gain some level of trust. If you are destined to become close and have a true friendship, that's great. Such friendships will always start with little things that take on importance if you stay aware and pay attention.

People in management positions seem to miss this piece of the puzzle on occasion. They sometimes say, "Well, this person works for me; therefore, we don't need to build a relationship that has a personal element, because we already have a professional relationship." Or, they will think, "I probably won't ever need this person in my life, so I don't need to know who he or she is." In contrast, my approach is that I want to know something about everybody I meet because I never know how our lives might be brought together and *you never know when you are going to need a relationship.* I may be able to help one person some day. At some point down the road, somebody may be able to give me some important advice, or put me in touch with someone who can assist me. *This is a proactive, versus reactive, approach to building relationships.*

The best way to successfully network and meet people is when you're happy and content with yourself. It's hard to connect with people who are negative and down because they will influence you in a negative way and more often than not, they won't be open to building new relationships. You've got to be at peace with yourself. There have been times in my life when I wasn't happy. I was selfish and things weren't going the way I wanted them to. I tried to force situations, which didn't work out. Finally, I realized that I couldn't control all external circumstances and external factors. I simply can't control the things I can't control. All I can do is be the best person I can be and try to meet the best people I can meet. If I give to people in my community and I'm really sincere about it, I'll reap rewards in surprising ways.

The goal of *Get Off the Bench* is to make you, the reader, an effective networker. I want to open your eyes to valuable concepts and techniques and show you how to use networking, so that it works for you. If you would like to merge your instincts for success and human interaction, and make the whole of your life worth more than its combined parts, then what I explain and discuss in these pages should appeal to you. If you read them and consider them, then, in time, you will become a competent networker without any sense that this mode of interaction is not your natural way. I hope, and even expect, that this will be the case.

Disclaimer: This book is based solely on my own personal experiences of success and failure, trial and error, and taking risks and trying new approaches. It is not based on scientific research, analysis, or experimentation.

THE VALUE OF RELATIONSHIPS

CHAPTER ONE

"Curious people are interesting people. I wonder why that is."
—*Bill Maher*

I was the first person in my family to go to college. It was a strange feeling to leave New Orleans, head west to Louisiana State University (LSU) in Baton Rouge, and hope for the best. Later, it was even stranger when I arrived in Washington, D.C., after my college graduation: I was the new person in town and hardly knew a soul. My focus was on learning a new job and becoming skilled in my profession. At the same time, I already felt the importance of building a new network of people with whom I would be close and get along—people I could help, who might someday help me.

Such a challenge is the same in any town, but it is especially challenging in big cities, like Washington, D.C., where there's transience. In places like this, people come in for a few years and then they leave—they get transferred or they pursue an opportunity somewhere else. The desire or the time required to make relationships doesn't always exist. Conversely, in New Orleans, I had been friends with young people whose fathers were friends with my father. Even our grandfathers were friends with each other.

When I say it's important to know people and create a comfortable, social feel in interactions, that doesn't mean I always understood these points. I haven't always been an outgoing or confident person who put everyone at ease. In fact, it took me a while to learn the right personal style in business environments. I believe part of the reason for this was because formative professional years took place when I was working at the CIA during the 1980s and 90s. At that time and place, President Ronald Reagan and CIA Director William Casey set the tone. One thing about the CIA and its new recruits— they throw you right into the thick of things. I went from college to the CIA overnight and was given enormous responsibility. After I left the CIA, I had to realize that not everything was a mission, not everyone followed orders, and that not everyone was cut from the same cloth. I had to modulate my approach and personality so it was more attractive and welcoming to those around me. I've always had a naturally aggressive and no-nonsense personality but didn't always show my humorous or compassionate sides. I had to learn new ways of handling and managing myself so people felt comfortable and I didn't turn them off or drive them away.

People matter to other people. We are a social race. We are geared toward productive work and focus on measurable outcomes, yet even with this focus we ultimately cannot ignore the powerful element of human connection. It takes more than just being smart or going to the right schools to succeed. Being successful in the business world, or in any environment for that matter, requires that each of us have the ability to effectively engage with people, build relationships, and become part of larger circles.

The thing about people is that we all want to matter. We all generally want to achieve. We want to leave footprints—we want to make our mark. Whether we realize it or not, we are striving to be relevant and significant. The defining characteristic of human relevance is the ability to treat others as we'd like them to treat us. Fortunately (or unfortunately, depending on your point of view), whether or not we matter—whether or not we are relevant—is in the eye of the beholder. We tend to define our success in terms of how others view us.

Given the above, why is it that so many managers and executives in today's business world seem to invest so little time in building personal and strategic relationships? Simply put, I think this is caused by a lack of awareness: *people sometimes lack awareness of the importance of relationships.* By not valuing personal and strategic relationships, these executives hurt their own causes. They miss business opportunities, are not considered for job promotions, and are being denied access to critical information flow, which is vital to personal and professional success.

So, what are these types of networks? Let's define a personal network: it's a fabric of intrinsically valuable friendships that enhance one's pleasure in life. By contrast, we define a *strategic* network as a carefully planned web of cooperative social relationships that don't just happen by accident at the water cooler. Strategic relationships are powerful because their goal is to actually create value for all involved.

Moreover, strategic networks, especially at the business community's senior executive level, control the flow of and access to sensitive and critical information. Members of a strategic network typically exchange information based on their pooled knowledge and experience. There is one more piece: strategic network members are also often times connected to each other through their *personal* networks. Therefore, those wanting to gain access to the network's information, or gain access to certain people within the network, must strategically build and leverage their own networks to do so.

I'm not talking about "using" people, or some sort of mercenary use of networks here. Instead, I'm talking about cultivating genuine relationships—friendships, if you like—that must be nourished and tended with great care and greater discretion.

Thus, this book's foundation is formed on two hypotheses:

1. Strategic relationships are powerful and tangible assets with real value and should be nurtured, protected, and invested in; you should treat them as you would anything of value.

2. When others feel comfortable with you (when they trust you and enjoy your company) and have confidence in your abilities, you will find that opportunities begin to appear.

Let me say, at the outset, that while many of my stories and examples center around business executives due to the fact that I've been in the business world for many years, the principles I discuss in this book are universal; they apply to anyone. Indeed, they apply to anyone who has to interact with other people in any capacity. In this book, I do not prescribe anything that is beyond the capacity of anyone who has a little grit, drive, and determination.

You don't have to have a gregarious, outgoing personality in order to build and maintain healthy, mutually beneficial relationships. I'm not here to do the equivalent of advising an aspiring basketball player to grow to seven feet tall. I'm here to help you develop into an effective networker without overhauling your natural personality. Even if you are a person of few words, there is an excellent networking technique and style you can take advantage of, and I'll provide you with a prime example later in the book. So, in general, what you will find in this book are practical tips and proven advice that anyone can use to develop a powerful and fruitful relational network.

Remember, strong, fruitful relationships are generally based on the idea of *quid pro quo*—giving something to get something. That's not a good or a bad thing; it's just the fact of the matter. During my long career of developing friendships and business relationships, I have witnessed a wonderful phenomenon: some people give because it's the right thing to do, or perhaps because they believe it is more blessed to give than to receive. We should stick with that phenomenon as the rule, not the exception. You have to bring something to the table. You have to have something to offer and you must be willing to offer it. Usually, that something is eminently practical and tangible.

Ultimately, this book is about creating strategic and business relationships, and developing those relationships for a specific purpose, with a specific end in mind. The book is about building a network that will help you meet your goals and objectives in business and in life. It is about unleashing the power of relationships to reach a particular, defined end. It is about one of the most important skills in a senior executive's portfolio: networking.

In addition to the two hypotheses that form this book's foundation, three fundamental maxims underlie it:

1. *When you need a relationship, it's too late to build it.* You have to create and foster relationships before they become necessary.

2. *It is more blessed to give than to receive.* Relationships are about give and take. Too often we take and don't give as much in return.

3. *Trust is the currency of all relationships.* Without trust and integrity, relationships, and therefore, a true network, cannot exist.

That said, now we will turn to the power of strategic networking, and how it can help you get the most out of your life.

TAKEAWAYS FROM CHAPTER ONE

- All people, with all types of personalities, have the ability to become successful networkers.
- Real relationships have value and should be treated as such.
- Strategic relationships are generally based on quid pro quo: each party brings something to the relationship the other party needs.
- When you need a relationship, it is too late to build it.
- Trust is the currency of all relationships.

NETWORKS AND NETWORKING: WHY SHOULD WE CARE?

CHAPTER 2

"When you need a relationship, it's too late to build it."
—*Dr. Lois Frankel*

You may be asking yourself, "Why should I care about networks and networking? It strikes me as a lot of effort and a lot of time away from the family. What's in it for me? Convince me."

I suggest another approach. Instead, you might ask yourself, "How many times have I missed an opportunity because I didn't even know it existed? How many times have I not been asked to be part of something because I wasn't known well enough? Why do I keep getting passed over for promotions?"

Given the global economy's trajectory over the past few years (and the worrisome trends in unemployment, home foreclosures, and loan defaults), the strategic network's power and resources have never been more critical in helping those in need. *Navigating through these challenges is nearly impossible without a network.*

POWER, INFORMATION, AND ACCESS

Networking is strategic. It is also about bringing value to a relationship. When value isn't exchanged, a potential relationship remains nothing more than two people meeting. The vital difference between just meeting new people and networking is twofold:

1. Networking involves planning, investment, and follow up.
2. Networking is about finding out how you can offer value to others and how they can offer value to you. In contrast, simply meeting people involves an introduction, a handshake, or perhaps an exchange of business cards. It ends there.

Let's examine this from a technical perspective, using the analogy of a computer network. Your computer is usually connected to a network. When you ping the network with a request, generally a request for information, you begin a bilateral process. For example, suppose you send a command to your computer to pull up a particular website. The network processes your request, finds what you're looking for, and then sends it back to you. The network moves information back and forth. Yet that's not all. That network controls information. If you don't have the correct address or the permissions (i.e., access), you can't get information to or from a particular part of the network.

Next, think of a stand-alone computer: one that is not tied to a network. It can only draw from its internal resources. Such a computer may be very powerful and have many stunning applications. Yet in the end, it is vastly inferior to a networked computer from the standpoint of information and resource access.

Human beings are the same way. Those who are not "plugged into" a network can only draw from their own resources. They may be highly talented; however, in the end, they are limited from an access standpoint and, therefore, they are also limited in their capabilities. Conversely, people who are plugged into networks can draw on an almost infinite number of resources and have access to more data that will help them reach their goals. *Their power expands exponentially.*

However, take this word of caution about networks. *In any networked environment, there is always the danger of a virus.* One bad apple can indeed spoil the whole barrel. Therefore, it is critical that each person you allow into your network be vetted. Ensure the members of your network reflect your values, ethics, and objectives. Other people can tell a lot about folks by whom they associate with, so be judicious in deciding which individuals to allow in your network.

Ultimately, the network provides power, opportunities, information, and access—all of which are critical for business world success.

HOW THE BUSINESS WORLD WORKS TODAY

Today, a fair number of people wonder why they're not on management's radar, not moving along the career path, not getting invited to the popular events and parties, or not getting opportunities for bigger positions and really plum jobs. Most often it's not a matter of skill and competence, or lack thereof. Rather, it's because influential people don't know them; either they don't have a reason to know them or they don't know them well enough to feel comfortable putting them into leadership positions or bringing them into their network. They are simply not on the radar of those making critical decisions about hiring, developmental assignments, and advancement.

Achieving success is not only about how smart or talented you are; it's also about the people you know. In the real world, corporate board members do not say, "Okay, we need a new CEO for our Fortune 100 Company. Someone great might be out there. We'll scan major metropolitan areas and come up with 200 resumes." It just doesn't work that way most of the time. Instead, people hire people they know and trust. At the senior level, it is about who you know and, more to the point, *who knows you.*

However, who you know and who knows you are not a substitute for personal value and substance. Even with great connections, you must excel at what you do. *Networks don't replace energy, integrity, and competence.* You can't be a successful networker if you're a bullshit artist. People don't typically want to network with someone who's too slick or doesn't come across as genuine. I can't tell you how many times I've gone to a business function and had people I don't know shove business cards in my face, asking me to do something for them. Those requests fall on deaf ears because I didn't, and don't, know those people, so I can't vouch for them. *Vouching for someone means putting your name and reputation on the line.*

Let's face it, you've got to do more than just act loud and aggressive. You've got to put yourself out there so people take notice of you for the *right reasons (please refer to Appendix B for more on this topic).* You need to be outstanding in your field, and you also need to be known, trusted, and vetted. Ask yourself, "How large and diverse is the population of effective people who know me?" The next question is, "How comfortable are people with me?" Recall this book's second premise: *When others feel comfortable with you, when they trust you, enjoy your company, and have confidence in your abilities, opportunities will begin to appear.* At the highest levels, who you know and who knows you become increasingly vital to your continued success. It is simply the way business is done; it is how the world works.

Still, some people think that because they have a special skill or a degree from a top-notch school, and a job opening requires that skill and education, they should get the job. Unfortunately, that's naïve.

Skill and ability are the antes that get you into the game. They're table stakes. Once skill and ability are a given, then you're competing against similarly qualified people who know—and are known by—the people who will influence hiring decisions.

For example, I was talking to a friend of mine recently about a government agency official. This official, a deputy director, was bemoaning the fact that he had always been the deputy and was never going to be the senior guy. My friend told him that the reason the deputy would never be considered to be a senior guy is because he wouldn't do anything beyond his job. He didn't go to any conferences or holiday events, and he didn't go down to Capitol Hill to meet people. He just went to his office, did his work, and went home. "That's why you've never become the boss," my friend told this deputy director. "That's how things work. It's not good or bad—it's morally neutral—it's just a fact."

How the World Used to Work

In America's not-too-distant past, people typically stayed loyal to one corporation for their entire careers. They entered at a junior level and perhaps worked their way up the corporate ladder into management. If they were lucky, worked hard, and played their cards right, they made it into the executive suite. It wasn't unusual for employees to retire from companies that had hired them when they were fresh out of college.

In turn, corporations were loyal to their employees. They provided stable and relatively secure environments. While meeting people outside their own companies was not overtly discouraged, such networking was not really necessary: the companies provided internal social interaction. IBM, for example, had monthly dinners for employees, who were expected to show up with their spouses for the gatherings. IBM also provided employees with country club memberships. That's company-level—what we'll call *operational networking*, or done-for-you, molded-by company culture.

In contrast to operational networking, relationship networking, while a relatively new term, is not a new concept. In the recent book *The Art of the Network: Strategic Interaction and Patronage in Renaissance Florence*, Paul D. McLean suggests that Renaissance Florentines could rely on "codified behaviors by means of which to draw out those willing and able to be friends." The behaviors I'm discussing descend directly from those behaviors. Yet the Florentines did not invent such behaviors. Select groups and societies that form tight knit networks have existed since early human history.

Throughout human history, the power elite has formed its own network. The common phrase for this is the "old boys' network." To facilitate these networks, the young scions of great families were educated along with their peers. These young men become lifelong friends, and for all intents and purposes, form a network. In the United States, these relationships were forged on prep school playgrounds and Ivy League college campuses. These people made decisions that affected the nation in smoke-filled backrooms. They were in a tightly knit club that was simply not open to outsiders.

Fortunately, the United States was founded on democratic principles. Many of our forefathers were Freemasons, people who cultivated an extraordinary level of strategic networking. Democracy has a great leveling effect. The natural aristocracy is no longer a closed system. We have become, to some extent at least, a meritocracy. In a meritocracy, anyone can rise to prominence. There are, of course, still closed systems within the meritocracy. Two examples are the University of Virginia's Seven Society and Yale's Skull and Bones. The fact is, even as our world transforms to a more open, global, and connected place, networks remain as powerful as ever.

At this point, we should also note the impact technology has had on networking, especially in recent years. Technology has had a great leveling effect: it has made networking that much easier, and that much more democratic. Anyone with access to the web can be connected to anyone else on the planet who is also connected to the web. All this takes is the use of sites like LinkedIn, Facebook, and Twitter. This is a mind-boggling reality but, as we shall see in a later chapter, an eminently real one.

WHY SOME PEOPLE DON'T NETWORK

There are three main reasons why people don't network:

1. *They don't understand the value of networking.* Some people don't network because they just don't understand, realize, or appreciate the importance of people. They undervalue relationships and fail to see the necessity of networking. They may believe they can get by on their skill set, charisma, or their intellect alone. They prefer to play the lone wolf, but come across as arrogant and distant. This is a sad miscalculation.

2. *They don't want to network.* Other people just plain aren't interested in networking. It seems like too much work; they don't believe they have the time for it; or they fear they lack the personality traits to network effectively. I know some people who can't separate work and life boundaries, so, to them, networking represents the ultimate challenge of keeping their professional and personal lives separate, and they avoid it. In these situations, I encourage people

to allow the two parts of their lives to intersect. When networking, you still have to dutifully manage your time, as you would in any other situation. However, I believe allowing your networking life and your personal life to overlap occasionally can be very beneficial.

3. *They don't know how to network.* Finally, there are those who would like to network and who accept the importance of networking, but don't know how to do it. They lack a networking model, techniques, and honestly wonder how to go about it. Given guidance, people in this category may flourish or they may feel too uncomfortable approaching people and fade off the radar.

NETWORKING IS TEACHABLE AND REPEATABLE

There are four types of networkers:

1. *Power networkers* include most politicians. They're out every night, going to dinners, going to events, and developing relationships. They are very strategic about networking and engage with high and sustained energy. These types of networkers need to be careful not to be overbearing. They can alienate an audience or saturate the market with their presence.

2. *High-impact networkers* operate at a lower level of intensity than power networkers. Nevertheless, they have a strategic approach to networking that massively improves their effectiveness.

3. *Moderate-impact networkers* network both inside and outside their current organizations with high levels of intensity; however, they use a networking approach that

is more tactical than strategic, which limits their overall networking effectiveness.

4. *Low-impact networkers* engage in networking when and where they feel entirely at ease. They are never willing to leave their comfort zones.

Ask yourself: where do I fall on this spectrum?

While networking is certainly easier for people who seem to be naturally equipped with ideal networking personalities, everybody can improve their networking abilities if they really want to. This improvement requires commitment and determination. It involves tactics, techniques, and procedures based on fundamental principles of human interaction that are easily learned, repeatable, and simple to put into practice. In addition, because networking principles are teachable and repeatable, no one is excluded from the proverbial club when practicing those principles.

Thus, the first Law of Networking is a corollary to something you may have learned in high school physics, the Law of Conservation of Mass: *What you put into the system, you get out of the system.*

This is similar to the computing analogy: garbage in, garbage out. If you put little effort or low quality service into the system, you will get little effort or low quality service from it. You must strike a balance between subject matter expertise and networking expertise.

THE NUMBER ONE SOURCE OF OPPORTUNITIES AND CHOICES

Your network's size and effectiveness is inversely proportional to your risk of missing important opportunities and directly proportional to your exposure to important opportunities. A strong network will not only mitigate the risk of unfulfilled potential; it will also open up many new opportunities. Many, perhaps most, opportunities to meet people, to serve on boards and panels, to find plum jobs, and to go to events all come about through the people you meet. Having a strong network opens up a whole universe of possibilities for you, both personally and professionally.

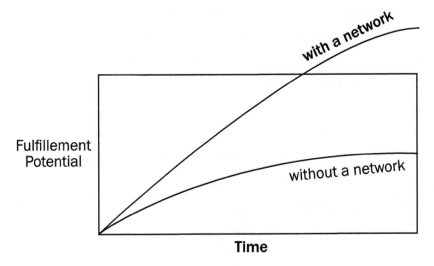

Figure 1: The Potential for Fulfillment is Greater with a Network

Having a productive network is about getting to experience life at its fullest. It's also about having a say in how things turn out; in other words, *having a say in managing the outcome*. Figure 1 depicts a graph of the Life Fulfillment Curve: the curve is shown both with and without a network. As you can see in Figure 1, without a network, you might achieve about half of your potential. Eventually, your opportunity for fulfillment will level off. In contrast, with a network, you can figuratively go off the chart in achieving fulfillment and reaching beyond your anticipated potential. In such cases, fulfillment is only limited by the constraints you place on yourself and the network.

Think of it this way: if you don't have a network, *you're at the mercy of other people.* For example, a friend of mine was recently laid off from a company she had been with for fourteen years. She knows no one and is struggling to find a job. She doesn't have a clue about which people to talk to or how to go about taking the first step in finding a new job. In her situation, others are controlling her destiny. She doesn't have the network or the support system to help her weather the storm.

People who operate and venture outside their comfort zones are networking, whether they would use that word or not. Their relationships aren't defined by jobs. They make a point of networking with *dissimilar* people. So, emulate them. Don't be solely concerned with the sheer number of contacts you have. *Instead, think quality over quantity.* Develop a diverse network of relationships. That's quite different from developing the same relationship dozens of times over. Think of the old adage: *do you have twenty years of experience, or one year of experience twenty times?* The same principle applies to networking. In order for your network to be effective for and advantageous to you, diversity is key.

An Executive's Job IS to Network

There are NO effective executives who don't network. An integral part of the executive's job is to network. This may be an unwritten rule: it may remain unspoken, and it may not show up on your job description or your performance review. Still, do not be deceived by this. Networking is expected and necessary for getting things done. As an executive, you do have to be a leader, accomplish your goals, deliver on your mission, and execute. Thus, a vital part of your job is knowing people who can get things done and help you achieve your (or your organization's) goals. Your responsibility is to nurture productive and mutually valuable alliances, friendships, and business relationships. Translation: this means you need to *network consistently and constantly.*

More and more, recruiters' job specifications say things like: "The candidate must be highly connected within senior levels of the customer community," or "The candidate must be well connected on Wall Street and with the investment community." It is a common requirement that candidates for leadership positions in any organizations be thoroughly plugged in to the appropriate network(s). The folks running organizations realize that they need individuals who know people and have strong networks in leadership roles. The higher you go up the ladder, the more your network plays a key role in your success.

MULTI-LEVEL CONVERSATIONS

Conversations between CEOs—or between any senior executives with major responsibilities—are different in form and content from conversations that take place between individuals below corporate levels. In a typical conversation between two CEOs who have not met before, more than half the time is spent discussing the community or industry they are in. Say you're sitting next to them in a restaurant. You'll hear them discuss industry trends and initiatives. Then, they'll move to an overview of people they've worked with in the past and discuss how they can leverage their relationships to make things happen. Talking about whom they know and revealing their opinions of different people tells them more about each other than almost any other topic would. People are always the subtext of these conversations.

Discussing resumes at the executive level is, frankly, boring. Education, for example, is cut and dried, while experiences and jobs speak for themselves. A CEO might think, "Well, this candidate earned his master's degree from a reputable school and has a good track record, so he's clearly got skills." It's much more interesting and telling to hear a candidate's answers to the following questions: "What do you think of so-and-so? Do you think he can keep up with you? Can she get things done? Could he make a phone call on my behalf to get something done?" That's the discussion at the CEO level.

What's important to you—when you're at an organization's lower levels—is not always important to the people higher up in the organization. I've had a discussion about this with my peers over and over. When we were younger and at lower levels at our respective organizations, we always believed we could see situations clearly and understand what needed to happen. We'd think, why can't the boss see things like we do? Why isn't he doing anything about it? Then one day, we became the bosses and realized that, as the boss, *there are pieces of the puzzle that you have but others don't.* Remember, the higher your position, the more information you have to take into account when making decisions, and the more stakeholders you have to be concerned with. As a CEO, I talk about things very differently than I did when I was a vice president or a director. When you're a VP or director, you're networking and meeting people who are professionally senior to you. So, you need to be able to have discussions in the context of what's important to them and understand what is influencing them.

For example, there are young people who want to network with me, but they talk about things that do not interest me or that I do not know about. I will certainly be courteous and listen to them, but in the end, we usually don't make a strong connection. We are on different frequencies. The people who impress me and get time with me are the ones who understand what's important to me and can speak to the things I'm keenly interested in. *Knowing what is important to your audience is important to making connections.*

SELF-DETERMINATION AND THE NETWORK

If you don't invest in relationships, you must accept the fact that you are at the mercy of circumstances. Failure to invest in yourself and others is akin to sacrificing the freedom to live as you choose on your own terms. When you don't know the right people, others will pretty much dictate what you can and can't do. In other words, having a network is about controlling your destiny, controlling your outcomes, and managing the things that you want to do. If you don't have relationships with anyone outside of your current organization, you are entirely at the mercy of the executives (or HR) who run your company. They can decide to lay you off, fire you, or marginalize you, all on a whim. Then what?

If you are connected and know people outside of your organization, then you have a safety net. If you get laid off, you can call your pal, a recruiter, and arrange your next job (refer to the emails earlier in the book). Often, people who have been laid off or fear being laid off look around and realize that they don't know anybody who can help them. By then, it is too late to build the necessary relationships that would form an effective safety net. It is astonishing that people don't seem to intuitively understand this principle. Remember maxim number one: *When you need a relationship, it's too late to build it.*

An example that demonstrates this point is that of executive recruiters. If you are properly networked and the recruiters do their homework, they will find you. If you need to find *them*, that is a sure sign you are not adequately networked.

In the last few years, I've lost count of how many people have reached out to me for help in finding a job, mostly because those people were not networked. The same goes for colleagues and recruiters who have contacted me regarding a potential hire's reference. In these cases, even when I am not listed as a reference, I may have a history with the person in question or we may have worked at the same company. I hope that the economic meltdown that started in 2008 has taught people in the workforce that avoiding networking is no longer an option.

Change happens. It is inevitable. Because of this, working on self-determination is preferable to being defenseless against the slings and arrows of outrageous fortune. Networking puts you in the driver's seat and allows you to design your future. With a network surrounding you, you won't drift aimlessly. Instead, you can seize the opportunities that will inevitably present themselves. *You will be in control and be able to manage the outcome.*

KNOWLEDGE-BUILDING AS A RESULT OF RELATIONSHIP-BUILDING

In a strong and effective network, people learn from each other continuously. Much of what we learn over the course of a career is not what we learn from our work or school. Instead, much of our learning comes from interacting with other people. Executives should be talking to investment bankers, attorneys, real estate agents, and engineers. They should have the occasional coffee with people from every industry so they can talk to those people about what they do and what's happening in their industries. This is important for a well-rounded executive; an executive needs to be a Renaissance person, at least on a small scale.

Ask yourself the question, "How many times in the last year have I needed or wished I had known somebody or been part of a group?" If the answer is that you don't have the relationships you need, you ought to think about how to begin networking and to start meeting people. Fundamentally, you need to see the value of relationships in order to achieve your goals. While you may need to invest significant time in order to nurture relationships, and such nurturing can be hard, the benefits far outweigh the cost. Once again: *When you need a relationship, it's too late to build it.*

TAKEAWAYS FROM CHAPTER TWO

- o   Networks offer power, information, and access.
- o   The world is a networked environment.
- o   Everyone can learn to network effectively.
- o   Understanding your audience is key to building relationships.
- o   Effective networking provides opportunities and choices.
- o   Effective networking allows for self-determination.

PREPARING TO BUILD YOUR NETWORK

CHAPTER 3

"It's not about who you know, but who wants to know you."
—*J.D. Kathuria*

As you prepare to build a network, remind yourself of the virtue of patience. The network-building process takes constant effort and the willingness to step outside your comfort zone, but the outcome is worth it. Networking can also be enjoyable: you're sure to meet some great people along the way. After all, the dedicated network-builder has to connect with people of all types. That takes well-developed social skills and the ability to read situations. How do you begin? This all starts with knowing yourself.

Knowing yourself means having an honest understanding of your reputation. People will judge you based on your accomplishments, your character, your integrity, your personal style, and what you bring to the table. They will wonder if a relationship with you will lead anywhere. So, you need to show them it will. It's up to you to know your goals and communicate the value you can bring to relationships. You must always have an endgame in mind.

YOUR REPUTATION

A reputation, like a professional network, is built slowly and steadily. As Benjamin Franklin pointed out: "It takes many good deeds to build a good reputation and only one bad one to lose it." You need to be very self-aware and understand how other people see you. Remember, a bad reputation is not easily mended. The best defense against an undeserved reputation is impeccable character. If you are a person of deep integrity, your reputation will not suffer easily. Remember that your performance and demeanor are constantly being discussed and measured. The best way to repair a damaged reputation is to demonstrate to those around you that you possess integrity, character, ethics, and can be trusted. Actions do speak louder than words and as a result, going out of your way to exhibit these desired traits is the only way to repair any damage.

A sales adage tells us, "The selling happens when you're not around." The same is true of building, or tearing down, reputations. Not everybody will be on board with who you are. Personally speaking, I know some people are not fans of mine, despite my best efforts to make them so. Maybe I made them mad or held them accountable (not everyone likes this, by the way); maybe we just didn't see eye to eye on an issue. I am fine with that outcome, as long as I know that I treated them respectfully and my integrity and character never came into question.

The circus master P.T. Barnum famously said, "All publicity is good publicity." In networking, the same doesn't hold true. People don't want to vouch for you if your reputation isn't solid. If you're known as someone who isn't trustworthy, who uses people, who is one-sided, or who doesn't bring a lot to the table, you're not going to have a very effective network. People aren't going to include you. Thus, avoid negative notoriety. It does not serve you well. As I mentioned in the introduction, *trust is the currency of all relationships.* Without trust, no relationships can exist. Without those relationships, effective networking is impossible.

On more than one occasion, I've been unpleasantly surprised by former associates' misguided requests for recommendations. Some of these requests are from people I had to terminate their employment for integrity violations. And they still want me to write them recommendations! Such people are not self-aware; they don't understand the importance of reputations.

BUILD YOUR BRAND

The number-one brand in the world is Coca-Cola. Its trademark is instantly recognizable the world over. Like Coca-Cola, you are a brand. Decide on your brand and build it. What do you want to be known for?

For example, I want to be known as a person who makes decisions and gets things done with integrity and ethics: someone who leads and makes hard decisions required for a team's success. I want people to know I won't shy away from a calculated risk and I don't operate based on fear of failure. Why don't I fear failure? I put it in the category of "the cost of doing business." Failure is inevitable, so it should be embraced rather than shunned. You can't hide from it. I want to be known as someone who is high-energy, works hard, drives people to do their best, and takes care of them when they do.

So, once you've established what you want to be known for, how do you build your brand? Generally, your brand or reputation is built over time by who you are, how you act, where you show interest, how you dress, how you speak, and so forth. Here are some specific criteria that influence how your brand is created:

- *Your interactions with others.* Are you calm and managed or impulsive and out of control? Do you let others speak or do you dominate the conversation? Do you use foul language or do you choose your words carefully? At social functions, do you remain in control or let alcohol take over?

- *Where you focus your time.* Do you spend more time at work than at home? Do you give your time to charitable causes? Do you take night classes or executive education classes? Do you spend more time on the golf course than in the office? Are you a workaholic who spends eighty hours a week at the office?

- *Your personal style.* Are you neat and orderly or just the opposite? Do you dress appropriately or is your attire sloppy? Do you smile or frown? Do you engage in conversation or avoid it? Are you a jokester or a serious person? Do you balance family and work or do you sacrifice one for the other? Do you ride a motorcycle or drive a "green" car? What are your hobbies?

- *Your leadership style.* Do you always deliver results or just create a lot of activity? If you manage people, are you an enabler or inhibitor? Do you spend time networking and attending required functions? Do you take risks or play it safe? Are you loyal? Do you have integrity? Are you an entrepreneur or a bureaucrat? Do you publish works or are you considered a "thought leader"?

Revealing who you really are will determine how people perceive you. If you are not genuine and down-to-earth but try to come across that way, people will pick up on the mismatch. *The best way to achieve your desired brand is to become the person you want to be through hard work, investing in yourself and others, and honest reflection.*

WHAT DO YOU BRING TO THE TABLE?

When I say, "What do you bring to the table?" what I am really asking is how do you sustain your network. My network consists of everybody from retired former executives to government executives and politicians to people who are just beginning their careers. And I'm fifty years old, so I'm in the middle somewhere.

As a CEO, my job is to deliver on the corporation's stated objectives while coaching, mentoring, and helping others in the organization. (See Appendix A for an article on mentoring, which I authored over ten years ago.) I'm happy to do it. In turn, people who are more experienced than me realize their job is to coach and mentor me. I can't be arrogant in either of these groups because the experts aren't going to have it and the novices won't appreciate it. In other words, being part of the network means I need to understand my place in the hierarchy. It's a natural hierarchy, not a chain of command. It's a network.

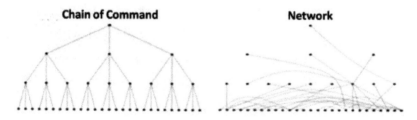

Figure 2. The Difference Between a Chain of Command and a Network

The traditional logistics supply chain works very much like the military chain of command, which is depicted on the left side of Figure 2. Here, each member of the network deals with or reports to only one other member of the network. There are no unexpected interactions.

Contrast that with the network depicted on the right side of Figure 2. In a network, novices can circumvent me and go straight to the experts. Can you pick out which member of the network might be described as the "king of networking" in that particular group? It's the one who sits third from the right, on the second row up from the bottom. That member is directly connected to seven other members. On a sitcom, his equivalent would be Corporal "Radar" O'Reilly from *M*A*S*H*. O'Reilly always seemed to bypass the chain of command by leveraging relationships with his wide and powerful array of contacts.

To the younger people in my network, I provide my expertise and access. Then, I go to the more senior people in my network to gain *their* expertise and access. With them, it's largely about me receiving, whereas with the younger people it's about me giving. No matter where you are, it's important to know what role you play in the network. Are you a provider and a mentor or are you a receiver and a student? That's a bit of a trick question. The answer is both, if you're networking effectively. This answer also demonstrates the *quid pro quo* of networking. I view networking *quid pro quo* like balancing a checkbook. You can make deposits and withdrawals, but it is important to keep a positive balance in the account. (These deposits and withdrawals come in the form of personal introductions, references, assistance, coaching, and so on.)

What else can you bring to the table on your mentors' behalf? Many senior executives serve on companies' boards and they are involved with other companies that need younger executives to advise, run operations, or identify talent. Sometimes the executives at these companies want to be plugged in to younger talent—people you know and can vouch for. They don't know everybody. Nobody knows everybody. That's where networking comes in.

Another thing I've been able to do for my mentors is get them on other companies' boards, in addition to the ones they already serve on. My wife and I take mentors out to dinner, just to spend time with them and meet their families. They come over for barbeques. We gather socially because we enjoy each other's company. If they need something—anything within my power—I will do it for them. For example, a friend and mentor emailed me recently because he needed contact information for a friend of mine. Of course I obliged, made the introduction, and connected them immediately.

However, it's not that my mentors continuously need things from me, although favors like the above do help. They appreciate knowing somebody who respects them enough to say, "You matter. I'd really like to learn from you because you know how it [whatever the subject in question is] all works." *For these relationships to succeed, both parties must have a certain amount of benevolence and mutual respect.*

YOUR GOALS ARE IMPORTANT

Do you know what you want out of life? Do you know where you want to be in five years? How about ten years? It's not enough just to know what your goals are. Do you have a strategic plan of how to get where you want to be and how to reach your goals? The fact is, your goals are attainable (That's assuming they are realistic, of course. For example, I will never play professional football because I can't plan myself into someone who's taller and faster!).Part of the beauty of the American Dream is that anyone can experience it. To gain your dream, set goals that are theoretically achievable. Then, figure out who can help you get there and accomplish those goals. Those who make the list will form the basis of your network.

EMOTIONAL INTELLIGENCE

To really understand the networking process, you've got to have emotional intelligence. If you look at people who've been incredibly successful and respected over a long period of time, you'll notice two things. One, they're extremely competent. Two, they lack outrageous egos—for the most part, that is. These successful individuals give their time to people who ask for it, but they don't let people take advantage of them either. Instead, they genuinely value people, understand talent, and know what drives performance. Simultaneously, they tend to be self-effacing, they know what they don't know, and they can take a joke. In other words, they're grounded and centered people. This doesn't mean they don't have healthy egos. A successful person's personality includes a healthy ego that's kept under wraps.

When networking, you'll meet all kinds of people and personalities. Some of these people may be successful, but arrogant: they think the sun rises and sets on them. They don't care about others. While they might say they care, the reality is they use people. Those who lack emotional intelligence, situational awareness, or emotional maturity always respond with the question, "How is this going to affect me?" That's because ego and confidence are often confused with arrogance. In other words, competent and talented people have ego and confidence because they've been through situations in which they've been required to deliver and recognize the importance of other people. Arrogance comes from either forgetting how you became successful or claiming success without really having delivered on your promises. That's like claiming to be a rock star and without having any hit records!

While people like this can survive in a high-powered environment for a while, in the end they tend to self-destruct. They can fool people sometimes, but eventually they are unmasked. I've seen it happen dozens of times throughout my career. They are not achieving *sustained success*. Sustained success is hard and I respect those who can achieve it. It's a combination of skill, effectiveness, character, integrity, intellectual curiosity, and networking. (I address this topic in more depth in Appendix B).

Over the past fifteen years, I've known some rising stars who haven't succeeded as one would have expected them to. Instead, they have self-destructed—to the point that if they ever find another job, it'll be amazing. Members of the community have written them off for a variety of reasons. They either lack emotional intelligence, they don't care about people, or they've done stupid things, such as having inappropriate relationships at work, stealing from the company, lying to management, or playing favorites. While some of these people were in incredibly strong networking positions (or so they thought), when other members of the network learned what they had done, they shut them down. The network was no longer available to them.

At the end of the day, you'll be more successful if you genuinely care for others' welfare (not only for your own). If you're grounded, centered, and amass emotional intelligence about what's going on around you, you will go far. Remember, part of the premise of networking is that you have to bring something to the table that will help other people. People who lack that sort of ability aren't going into a networking situation with another party thinking, "How can I help you?" Instead, they're going in thinking, "What can you do for me?" While you can get away with that for a little while, you can't do so permanently; it's simply not sustainable. Selfishness is not a desirable or admirable executive character trait.

Still, some senior executives get to a level where they begin to take the "I've arrived!" approach. I have a different philosophy. When I became a CEO for the first time, I never thought, "I've arrived. I'm here. I've hit the big time," and stopped working. Instead, my reaction was, "The hard stuff is just beginning. I have a lot to learn and a lot to prove. I have a lot of people depending on me, so I better know what I'm doing." *Once you stop learning, you're done.* Life is no longer fun. I have friends in their seventies who used to be CEOs of major corporations and they still take classes at local universities—they continue learning. Now that's the right attitude.

NETWORKING AS A FORM OF POWER

There are various forms of power: political, financial, positional, and so forth. Another form of power comes from your network. You may be asking yourself, "How do I know when I've reached a level of success in building my network?" One way is to gauge how much influence (or power) you have with others inside and outside of your network.

For example, I know several people in the Washington, D.C. area who can influence just about anyone. This power comes from a combination of three things: the positions they've held in government or industry, their financial situations, and the people they know. Clearly, you can't influence people or outcomes if you lack reputation, credibility, and integrity. All three are required in order to make sure others listen to you, believe in you, want to help you, and follow your advice. All the elements of networking come together at this point.

Once you have created a network and a reputation that allows you to influence others, you must never abuse the privilege this provides. Such abuse happens all too often. For those who fall into this trap, they quickly find out that the network they had built up can be unforgiving—especially if they take unfair advantage of their situation. It is as important not to overuse your position or power as it is not to abuse it. Be careful to ensure you don't saturate your network with too many requests or directives. Be selective.

Let's stop for a minute and recap. Building a network and achieving your goals is sequential. First, build up your skills, reputation, and credibility. While you are doing this, plot your strategy, identify your targets, act, and follow up. By maintaining your network well, all of the following will be enhanced: helping others, leveraging your network, and improving yourself.

TAKEAWAYS FROM CHAPTER THREE

- Build your brand and reputation carefully. Think of yourself as a product or service and define how you want to be known and perceived.
- Emotional intelligence and situational awareness of your reputation, brand, and outside perceptions of you are critical to building your network.
- Understand your personal and professional goals before you set out to build your network.
- Building the network is a series of steps that must be completed in order to get the most out of it.
- Effective networks create power by allowing you to influence decisions and results. They provide you with insights, information, and opportunities you would not otherwise have.

SEEKING OUT A TARGET-RICH ENVIRONMENT

CHAPTER 4

"Why do you rob banks? Well, that's where the money is."
—*Willie Sutton, alleged*

Now we come to the crux of the matter: How do you target strategic networking opportunities? Where do you even begin?

Getting started is not nearly as complicated as it may seem at first. Selecting a strategy is largely dependent on your goals or objectives. What outcome are you seeking? What do you want to get out of the network?

While you're considering your answers to these questions, let me tell you how I began. I didn't start out with clearly defined and well thought out objectives. I didn't even know I needed them. I had my fair share of ambition as I started my career but wasn't sure how to take the first step beyond finding my first job after college. However, I was fearless and open to ideas and situations that would allow me to grow professionally and personally. I've always been fascinated by the elements of the truly successful career. I watch what people do to succeed or to self-destruct. Some things I want to replicate, while many things I want to avoid. I love to watch talent and I love to watch people succeed. Success factors thrill me.

I was very fortunate, during my early days in Washington, to have a great job that I enjoyed. Beyond that, my assets were minimal. I had few connections, I had no impressive pedigree, and I had no money. As I said, I didn't have a strategy for how I was going to develop a successful career and life. Then I discovered the Tower Club Tyson's Corner.

For several years during the late 80s and early 90s, every day on my way to work, I drove by the Tower Club in Tyson's Corner, Virginia. By the end of that time period, I was saying to myself, "I want to belong to that club." I wanted to join because of the people inside the club's walls. During the first technology boom (later known as the dot.com debacle) of the late 1990s, the Tower Club's membership list was a "Who's Who" of D.C.'s power elite: the list included CEOs, business executives, high-profile journalists, attorneys, politicians and high-ranking government officials.

At some point, I was able to grasp the obvious; if you're a member of the Tower Club, you gain access to the other members and achieve an automatic level of initial acceptance. You also get to learn from the membership and understand how they became successful in their careers. I still didn't fully understand the importance of networking. However, I soon realized that if I was going to have a chance at having a successful career in this town, I had to get plugged in to such a network. I had to meet folks who could point out the right opportunities to me, educate me, help me, mentor me, and guide me. I needed to be the student.

The Tower Club was the central target of my strategic plan. Why the Tower Club? Well, why did Willie Sutton rob banks? Because the banks were where the money was. Why the Tower Club? Because that's where the network was, and still is.

In 1998, I had been living in the Washington, DC area for about 11 years when I was working in McLean, Virginia. My first week at work, a coworker invited me to lunch—at the Tower Club! I couldn't believe my ears. "I'd love to go to the Tower Club," I said enthusiastically. "I've never been there."

So, we went to lunch. Frankly, I was in awe. In the very elegant place, everyone was dressed in suits and was behaving with extreme politeness. It was a far cry from the blue-collar, edgy environment I grew up in. I said to my friend, "Wow! This is really great."

Then she asked me if I wanted to join.

"Of course," I said, "I'd love to be a member."

So, she nominated me, I filled out the application, went through the vetting process, and was accepted. This certainly changed my networking status.

For anyone in Washington who is in business and wants to be where the deals are made, where networks are established, and opportunities are created, the Tower Club was—and still is—the place to be. The Club is still well known for its distinguished membership, high-profile events, forums, and activities for the business and social community. It truly is the center of gravity for networking and collaboration in the D.C. area. My membership there has allowed me to build an incredible network, create many new friendships, meet many wonderful people, and achieve several of my professional goals.

However, when it comes to networking, you don't necessarily need a "Tower Club." The great thing about networking is that you can do it any place where there are people: Rotary Clubs, Mardi Gras krewes, church, PTAs, and so forth. Any platform will do as long as there are others involved. *Networking targets and environments are everywhere. You just have to look for them.*

ONE THING LEADS TO ANOTHER

In 2000, The American Heart Association came to the Tower Club and said, "We need a young executive who can help run our big event at the end of the year." Each year, two thousand people attend this huge event, held at the Ronald Reagan Building. The Tower Club recommended me for the job. My initial thought was that it would be a great deal of work, but I didn't want to pass it up. I said, "Great! I will get to contribute my time to an important charitable event, meet a lot of people, and it'll be a fun experience." Planning this black tie event took a year.

While planning the event, I met a man who was supporting it through its silent auction. When we first met, we hit it off immediately, so we decided to grab lunch and talk. A Bush 41 appointee, he's a great guy with a tremendous sense of humor who's well connected. At that lunch, I told him I wanted to help him with his silent auction. "I'll get you plugged in to our charity ball," I said. "But I need your help too. I want to get involved in politics." Today he continues to be a very good friend of mine and as you will read later in the book, this relationship eventually became very important for several reasons.

All of this happened because I was a member of the Tower Club.

I'm reminded of this terrific quotation from Lewis Carroll: "If you don't know where you're going, any road will get you there." Know yourself. Know where you are and where you want to go, and you'll succeed.

TAKEAWAYS FROM CHAPTER FOUR

- Be strategic in identifying where and with whom you want to network.
- Invest in your identified targets and learn as much as you can about them.
- Don't be a mercenary. Build real relationships.
- Focus your efforts on places and groups where networking is facilitated.

BUILDING YOUR NETWORK

CHAPTER 5

"Make choices that give you more choices."
—*Sid Fuchs*

For me, the Tower Club was my strategic target of opportunity for networking. I wasn't focusing on anyone in particular at the Tower Club—I just wanted to surround myself with the types of people who belonged there. I wanted to learn how to be successful from the masters. My target could just have easily been an individual person. Determining a target, or targets, really depends on your strategic objective.

So now what? Where do we go from here? How do we engage? Well, for example, when I joined the Tower Club, I didn't know anybody. That's when my networking began in earnest.

I started by going to the membership orientation, where I met all of the people on the club's staff. I also met a few new club members. Very quickly, I realized that the way to network in this club—the way to take advantage of what it and its members have to offer—was to align myself with the staff. So, I asked myself what I could do to help them. There are 1,500 members, and given the club membership's demographic, those members can be demanding at times. Being on staff at the club, as a membership director, can sometimes be a thankless job. So, I made sure to chat up the staff, asking each of the five in attendance for their business cards.

On the way home from the orientation meeting, I bought thank-you cards. I wrote a handwritten thank-you note to each member of the staff that I'd met. Well, as you might imagine, this helped them all remember me. The next time I came to the club, each of them greeted me warmly, by name, and thanked me profusely for my thank-you notes. Writing the notes was a small gesture, but it meant the world to the recipients.

For my next move, I decided to join a committee. I told club members I'd be happy to do whatever would be most useful. They put me on the Membership Committee, which meant I worked to recruit and evaluate new club members. This proved to be fortuitous. I would highly recommend joining such a committee to people who have difficulty networking. It's the perfect place to put your efforts, as it gives you the opportunity to meet everyone who is even peripherally related to an organization.

After I'd worked on the Membership Committee for a while, club members asked me if I'd be willing to serve on the Distinguished Speaker Series Committee. Even though I had my doubts, I said, "Sure." After all, I didn't know any distinguished speakers. But I teamed up with a long-time, well-known, highly respected club member, and we were able to get several famous and fascinating people to come speak at the Club.

Certainly, by arranging and coordinating meetings, coming up with agendas, and assisting with membership, I was providing a service to the club. While I was doing all this legwork, I was deriving great satisfaction and benefit in terms of beginning to build my network. It was genuine quid pro quo; the club was helping me and I was helping the club.

After some time, during which I remained readily available to the staff, I became known as the "go-to guy." Members are always bringing opportunities to the staff, asking, "Do you know somebody who could do this or somebody who could do that?" The staff members always thought of me first because I was always eager to help. I was making an investment in the club and, in turn, the club's members and staff were helping me by providing me networking contacts.

That's how I became a valued member of the Tower Club. I could have gone to the Tower Club and just had lunch. End of story. Alternatively, I could have joined and never invested one bit into the club. To gain the most from my membership, I really had to invest in it, and put time into it, in order to see what was possible.

You can't go from zero to one hundred in one shot. I couldn't join the Tower Club one day and receive a federal appointment the next. I had to join the Tower Club and their committees, and then work on the Heart Association Charity Ball. Then, I had to go through the Bush 43 campaign and then get nominated and appointed to the National Defense University Board of Visitors. Only then, finally, did I put myself in a position to receive the federal appointment I set out to gain when I first met my friend whom I asked to help me get engaged in the political scene in Washington, DC. To get where I wanted to be, I had to complete five or six steps along the way. With each step, my network expanded.

Networking is not a quantum leap. You can't go from isolation to being someone everybody knows (except in Hollywood, perhaps). You've got to take it in increments. The longer you take to start that networking process, though, the harder it is. *Creating an effective network is a marathon, not a sprint.* You can't build your network overnight. It takes time. As the network grows, so does its value.

A NETWORKING FRAMEWORK

My experience with the Tower Club is instructive. However, what if I had never been invited to lunch there? What if I had never had the opportunity to meet the staff, send them personalized cards, join committees, and start helping out? What would I have done then?

Let's look at the process and framework of networking: that's the methodology that comes into play once you've identified the target. Remember, you can't go to the top people right out of the box. You have to build a network incrementally, in stages, by leveraging degrees of separation. I mean the steps listed below to be instructive, but clearly you should modify them as appropriate for your situation. Also keep in mind that not all networking is strategic or will have clear objectives.

1. Set your objective for what you want to achieve.
2. Create a scenario and develop your plan of action.
3. Locate your targets and venues.
4. Identify what you bring to the table and discover areas of common interest with the targets.
5. Consider which of your current contacts may have a connection to your target.
6. Engage your targets and begin building relationships with them.
7. Follow up and ensure the lines of communication stay open.

8. Cultivate your network and invest time and energy in it, as required, to ensure the relationships grow.

STEP 1. SETTING YOUR OBJECTIVE: CRYSTAL CLARITY OF VISION

In this initial step, ask yourself the following: what do you want to achieve? What is your endgame? The key to any good strategy is a crystal clear vision of the desired outcome. Once you've achieved clarity about your ultimate objective, it isn't difficult to back up and identify the necessary steps to make it happen. Your objective may be highly specialized—like acquiring a particular job or getting a particular promotion—or it may be simply to expand your sphere of influence and make more friends. It doesn't really matter *what* the objective is. What matters is that your objective be precisely defined. Any objective (assuming, of course, that it is ethical) is fine and legitimate. More to the point, you can achieve any outcome for your objective by using the network. Simply follow the steps listed above.

Not all networking requires you to have a specific target or goal in mind. In such cases, you are not doing strategic networking; you are doing casual networking. Both types of networking are valuable and should be used in the appropriate settings. For example, if you are attending a function without a specific goal or person you want to meet in mind, then the casual networking approach (in which you talk to many people just to meet them) is appropriate.

When I was working at Northrop Grumman, I was the president and CEO of a subsidiary, The Analytic Sciences Corporation (TASC). I decided to put together an advisory board of people that could help me build the company. I knew who I wanted to be chairman. This man, an intelligence community icon, was a former Senior Executive at the CIA. Today, he is a legend in the intelligence community and one of the most respected, beloved individuals in D.C.

I called him and asked him to lunch. During our meal, I said, "Sir, let's put together a board—and I want you to be chairman. We'll put together a panel of five or six men and women who can help the company achieve its goals and help our customers become successful."

I asked him to recommend a list of ten people and send it to me. Then we could discuss the list and prioritize. To my surprise and pleasure, he said, "Great!"

So, there I was, thinking to myself, "What on earth are you doing by tasking this guy, an established leader in our industry?" The truth of the matter is that he felt good about being involved. He wanted to be part of what we were doing. He appreciated being asked to contribute to an organization, a set of customers, and a mission that had been a critical part of most of his life. Given his breadth and depth of expertise, knowledge and stellar reputation of our industry, he was a natural choice for this leadership position.

He sent me a list by email. We prioritized the people named, and then decided on the top five. I knew two of the men. I didn't know the other three, but I wanted to know them because I knew they were well-respected, senior people who could be very helpful to our business and customers. I called them all. Each of them said, "I'd love to join the board!" We had done it. My esteemed colleague chaired our first board meeting, and I got to know him and the five other board members extremely well.

While I became friends with all five board members, I really clicked with two of them. After about a year of serving on the board, they began coming to me for help on different, outside projects. One of their friends needed a job, a government customer needed help, and so on. Of course, I helped them out. While I've never asked any of them for a favor directly, they've provided invaluable mentoring and counsel over the years, as well as prized friendships. Having access to their knowledge and experience has absolutely helped me throughout my career.

STEP 2. CREATE A SCENARIO: WORK BACKWARDS FROM THE GOAL

This step involves mapping out the milestones required to reach your objective. The easiest way to go about this is to begin with the endgame and work backwards. Start by figuring out the final link in the chain, which takes place before acquiring the objective. If your objective is getting a particular job, then you should ask, who makes the final hiring decision? If your objective is receiving a particular promotion, then you should ask, who makes the call? If your objective is to expand your sphere of influence, then you should ask, what are your intended contacts' profiles? The same type of mapping goes for selecting new friends. No matter what the desirable outcome is, you will find there is a final hurdle to achieving the goal. Identify that hurdle and work backwards from there, one link at a time, until you can locate your initial target.

STEP 3. LOCATE YOUR TARGETS AND VENUES

Your first target may be an individual or an organization. Either way, begin by developing your campaign plan. Be strategic and creative in working out the steps necessary to meet your target. Remember, this target is the first, and therefore the most vital, link in the chain that will ultimately lead to your objective.

For me, that first target was the Tower Club. My objective was to be surrounded by highly-successful people so I could understand what makes them successful, what makes them tick, and how they approach life. Some may say that my objective was not clear, but there is a difference between clarity and precision. While my desire to be around successful and powerful people was indeed clear, I'll agree that it wasn't very precise. However, *precision will come over time as you begin to form strategies and outcomes.* Think of it like going to college. I knew that I wanted to go to college (I had clarity), but wasn't sure what I wanted to study until I had explored several avenues (and hence, I developed a precise objective).

STEP 4. IDENTIFY WHAT YOU BRING TO THE TABLE AND DISCOVER AREAS OF COMMON INTEREST

No matter what, you have to bring something to the party. You've got to give your time, resources, or something else. People who don't want to give are pretty much on their own. They have to rely on their own, internal resources. Some people can go a long way with that approach. However, if you show me a very successful person, I'll show you someone who not only has a network, but gives willingly to that network. Success comes in many varieties, whether it takes place in business, government, science, non-profit organizations, religious institutions, or beyond. Those who are highly successful in their fields are likely to have networks. It's highly likely they have a group of people that they're plugged in to: people for whom they offer help and can receive help from as well.

For example, a church parish is a network. So are a squash club, a woman's affinity group, a golf club, a Moose Lodge, and a V.F.W. (Veterans of Foreign Wars) branch. Each is a network; each has its own needs and provides its own service opportunities. In your network, identify what you have in common with your targets, and then define how you can serve those targets. In my experience, providing a service is the fastest and easiest way to gain entrance to a network. It's also the most enjoyable. Remember, making a good first impression is key.

STEP 5. CONSIDER WHICH OF YOUR CURRENT CONTACTS MAY HAVE A CONNECTION TO YOUR TARGET

This brings us to what I call the "*Second Order Effect*." Suppose you and I are in a network together: we're friends, but there's really nothing special we can do for each other. At this point, to help each other, we can employ the Second Order Effect. What this means is I reach out to help one of your friends from another network, or vice versa. In other words, we do each other favors by assisting each other's friends from outside our own, shared network. This is a secondary benefit to networking. The Second Order Effect is about helping both people and organizations peripheral to the original and primary network. We expand, or connect, the networks by helping each other's external contacts.

Another secondary effect of networking works as follows: Because people know that I know a particular power broker, and they know we're friends, I gain credibility. I gain this credibility because people know this third person (the power broker) is not going to waste time with people who aren't the real deal. If the broker spends time with me—if people see us having breakfast together, for example—that's good for me.

LinkedIn is a great tool for finding out who is connected to whom because it provides first-, second-, and third-order connections, and shows what makes up those connections. Remember, when you ask a contact to make an introduction to another contact—someone who is outside of your network—*you should always explain why you are requesting the introduction and what you hope to achieve by meeting that person.* Such knowledge will help the requester frame an introduction and give the contact the proper context. Then, the contact can accept or deny the request.

STEP. 6 ENGAGE YOUR TARGETS AND BEGIN BUILDING RELATIONSHIPS

Now you're ready to put your plan into action. The first meeting with a contact is critical. You must be affable, considerate, and willing to learn. Do not go in with guns blazing, talking about your ultimate goals. Remember this simple fact: *your objective in the first meeting is to get a second meeting.* Don't try to "close" someone in the first meeting. Don't oversell yourself. Instead, start developing a relationship. You've got to build trust. A first meeting is almost like a first date, and it can be just as awkward as a bad date if you are harboring ulterior motives. Genuine interest in other people is essential. People know if you're not truly interested.

During your first meeting with anyone, you need to consider asking these three questions:

1. Is this a good time to talk?
2. May I ask you a question?
3. What can I do for you?

This third question is the key. When you ask it, you've got to be serious. You have to mean it. You should never go into a networking opportunity with the attitude of, "What am I going to get out of this?" Being in a network is about positioning yourself and about giving back in order to receive. You're creating an environment in which you have more options and more choices. You gain these options and choices because you know people (and by extension, you know of their resources), you know about opportunities, information, and situations.

During such meetings, always have business cards at the ready. However, always ask for the other person's card before handing over your own. All too often, people race about, shoving cards in others' faces. My approach is to say, "May I have your business card?" People love to be asked for cards. Then I'll say, "Here's one of mine if you like." Ask for a card first—before you give someone your card. I can't even guess how many times I've taken a card without ever being asked for my card. It feels kind of empty. Don't put anyone in that position.

Here are some things to consider when embarking on the first meeting with a target:

1. Remember, the object of the first meeting is to get a second meeting.
2. Therefore, don't try to "close" in the first meeting.
3. Be affable and confident, but don't oversell yourself.
4. Be more interested in the other's concerns than your own.
5. Ask how you can serve the other person.
6. Be prepared for rejection.

If you receive rejection, it may not necessarily be personal. Your contact may not be a polished networker; alternatively, he or she may not understand the rules of engagement for networking success. In addition, your contact simply may not have an interest in networking with you, which can happen to anyone.

STEP 7. FOLLOW UP: ENSURE THE LINES OF COMMUNICATION STAY OPEN

Follow up initial meetings with handwritten thank-you notes. It always amazes me when people don't take advantage of this gesture. Writing a note is such a simple task, yet the return on your investment is enormous. Sadly, I see more people going the email route for cards and notes. As a result, the handwritten note carries more weight today than it ever has. I recommend personalized stationery, as it adds an extra touch. When you have an interview with someone, meet someone new, or take a meeting, send a thank-you note. Just write it and pop it in the mail. That's all you need to do, and it will blow people away. Sending a note is how you'll stand out. It doesn't have to be a long, drawn-out memo—just a short expression of your thanks.

Little actions like this can have lasting effects. My good friend Bill passed away a few years ago. As one of my close friends, he'd attended my fortieth birthday party several years before. After the party, I had sent handwritten notes to everybody who'd been there to celebrate with me (a group of about thirty people). My message was simple: "Thanks for coming. I really enjoyed sharing my birthday with you. Thanks for the gift. I really appreciate your friendship." It was that easy.

A couple of weeks after Bill passed away, I had lunch with his widow; I wanted to see how she was doing. I was astonished to see she had brought me the thank-you note that I'd sent eight years previously. "You've still got that card?" I asked, stunned.

Her response was even more surprising, "It was Bill's favorite card. He'd kept it on his desk since the day you sent it to him. He said nobody had ever sent him a thank-you card before for just going to a birthday party. He thought about it every day."

Little things like that matter. People get misty about them. When you do something small like send a thank you card, you get their attention, and you show your sincerity. *They will remember you for the right reasons.*

STEP 8. CULTIVATE THE NETWORK AND INVEST AS REQUIRED, ENSURING THE RELATIONSHIPS GROW

Once you have made initial contact, followed up, and started to develop a relationship, the next item of business is to keep that relationship alive and well. You can't go to your network just when you need something. That's not like giving back. Think of the best networks as genuine friendships. Take the computer analogy once again. In the old days, you had to dial up your modem every time you wanted to connect to a network. You could only get precisely what you asked for, and you could only get it when you were plugged in. Today, computers are always on networks. You're on a network even when you don't need anything from the network. It's the same thing with relationships. You have to find a way to maintain relationships and keep people interested while maintaining interest yourself. This doesn't mean you have to see people every week; in the case of someone you're not really close to, for example, you should seek them out a couple of times a year. In the next chapter, we'll look at how to keep in contact and stay on the radar.

Now, you must ask yourself the following: "Am I willing to put in the effort to build an effective and strategic network? Am I able to commit to the steps necessary for developing and cultivating meaningful relationships?"

FINDING THE BALANCE

Many people have asked me, "Doesn't networking take up too much of your time? If it does, how can you do that to your family?"

Networking is all about balance. I could ignore opportunities to network and choose to be home every night. After all, I can't network all the time. Sometimes I don't want to be plugged in because I need to recharge my batteries. At other times, I simply don't want to go an event, but I have to attend because of my job. In short, I have days when I don't want to network and days when I do. I'm not maniacally focused or totally gung-ho about networking *all* the time. That's normal.

Networking is not about sacrificing all of your personal time. While you will sacrifice some, you must focus on finding the balance. You've got to figure out what's important. Ensure you have created pathways that give you *more* choices, not fewer choices.

Networking has a secondary benefit too: it provides opportunities that can enhance your family's lives. Because of my networking, my wife and children have been to places and met people they wouldn't otherwise have visited or met, respectively. Similarly, your networking efforts will provide your family with access to opportunities and experiences that will be helpful to them as they make decisions about their futures. These are the personal benefits of investing in a strong network, benefits that should be considered in tandem with sacrifices of personal time.

TAKEAWAYS FROM CHAPTER FIVE

- Be as clear as possible about your vision: know what you want.
- Begin with the end in mind and work backwards.
- Develop a strategic plan.
- Be articulate about what you can offer your network.
- Execute the plan and follow up with people.
- Be genuine and sincere at all times.
- Expect some rejection, but don't take it personally.
- Realize that building your network takes time and doesn't happen overnight.
- Send handwritten thank-you notes after important and/or initial meetings.
- Balance your personal and professional life and include networking where and when you can.

LEVERAGING YOUR NETWORK

CHAPTER 6

*"Give me a lever long enough and a fulcrum on
which to place it, and I shall move the world."*
—*Archimedes*

There are three types of non-financial "capital," as described by economists, that are earnable and spendable within social network frameworks: *relational capital, social capital,* and *political capital.* All three are continuously in play. To be an effective networker, you need to understand which capital situation you are in at any time. Knowing which type of capital environment you are operating in will help you understand people's intentions and objectives; the resources required to build the capital; and the amount of capital you (or they) are willing to use in order to reach an objective. Let's examine each of the three types.

RELATIONAL CAPITAL

As economist Robert B. Reich says, it is "still the case that the cost to businesses of attracting a new customer is much higher than the cost of keeping one." This is why one of the most important business assets is relational capital. According to Reich, "Relational capital is the cumulative investment of trust, experience, and knowledge that forms the core of relationships between businesses and their customers. Relational capital keeps customers from abandoning a commercial relationship." This excellent definition has as much to do with personal, individual relationships as it does with business-to-consumer relationships.

I would argue that you could alter Reich's statement to read, "It's still the case that the emotional cost to individuals of developing a new relationship is much higher than the emotional cost of maintaining an old one." Moreover, it is still true that relationships are based on cumulative trust, experience, and knowledge.

Please don't think I am implying that you reach a point when it is time to close the door on building new relationships and merely work to maintain your current ones. Absolutely not. To close the door and stop expanding your network is a death knell for it. Close the door and you close the system.

Like everything else in the universe, relationships tend to break down over time unless acted on by outside forces. Consider a teacup that falls to the floor and smashes into a hundred pieces. That is entropy: it's the natural order of things. It is most natural for a teacup to shatter, if it falls. What doesn't happen in nature is that the shattered pieces reform into a perfect teacup. That only happens in a film that is being rewound. While a very talented and patient individual can recreate the teacup by using glue, the restored teacup will never be quite the same as the undamaged original. Like silver that tarnishes without polishing, houses that decay without attention, and teacups that shatter when dropped, relationships must be properly minded, lest they take the natural course and deteriorate. Relationships require constant vigilance.

How can you contribute to this vigilance? Well, you earn spendable relational credits by serving those in your network. As I mentioned earlier, think of this as a checking account: you make deposits and withdrawals in the network, and the end goal is always to end up on the positive side of the ledger. When you do a favor for someone in your network, you have accumulated capital that can later be spent. You may have done that favor out of genuine goodwill, expecting nothing in return, but the reality is that you have earned a credit. In a properly functioning network, everyone is accumulating a vast wealth of relational capita land they are never spending it wastefully or without deep consideration.

SOCIAL CAPITAL

Social networks have value. The difference between social capital and relational capital is that social capital is based on who you know (the relationships' quantity), whereas relational capital is based on how well you know people (the relationships' quality).

In other words, the network itself is a value-producing entity. C-suite recruiters are often, to be blunt about it, looking to hire someone with a great Rolodex (if anyone remembers what that is). Your connections to others are of superb value in the world. This is true not only in business and politics, but also in education, philanthropy, the arts, and just about any other field of human endeavor. The people you know matter. I know it sounds unrefined, coarse, and even a touch mercenary, but it is true. Rather than moralize about it, harness the power of social capital and let it work on your behalf. Let it help you achieve personal and professional fulfillment.

POLITICAL CAPITAL

Political capital is probably the least refined and most abused of the three types of network capital. As mentioned above, the first network type, relational capital, describes the strong bonds of trust between individuals and the value thereof. It describes the relationships' *quality*. The second type, *social capital*, describes the network's scale, footprint, and corporate value. In other words, it describes the *quantity of relationships*. Unfortunately, unlike the other two, political capital's close association with business and government taints it. Therefore, political capital often has an unsavory aspect.

Unlike relational capital, political capital is earned for the express purpose of spending with abandon. The purpose of gaining political capital is to wheel and deal, regardless of the quantity or quality of the relationships involved. Political capital can be described by the proverbial phrase, "You scratch my back and I'll scratch yours." While it may sound unfavorable, political capital is as essential to a fully functioning network as relational and social capital are. That's how the world works. While relational capital is based on trust (and sometimes even friendship), and social capital is based on the network's breadth and scale, political capital's express purpose is to move an agenda forward by leveraging relationships, position, power, or financial situation.

Significantly, the three types of capital do not exist independently of each other. They are always intertwining and mixing, as required by the given situation. Understanding which type of capital is in play at any given time, what types of withdrawals and deposits are being made, and, most importantly, what the limits and boundary conditions of those exchanges are, is critical. For example, you run the risk of damaging relational capital if you see it as purely political capital. Conversely, you stand to get tricked if you think you are in a relational capital situation (where trust exists), when you are really in a political capital situation (where trust is not always required).

Throughout the United States, "political capital" refers chiefly to the public goodwill politicians get to spend on their pet projects. The term finds its way into this book because, in a political network, political capital is very real, spendable currency. This has applied to almost every presidential administration in American history. (Lincoln's extraordinary "Team of Rivals" is a notable exception.)

A good example is Obama's presidency. After being elected President in November 2008, Barack Obama's first task was to put together a Transition Economic Advisory Board, which he did with vigor. He assembled a highly impressive cast of luminaries to guide him in his early decision-making. Most of these economic stars had come into his orbit only within the last few years—in fact, he had met the vast majority after entering the U.S. Senate in 2004. All seventeen board members shared an important characteristic: they did not need Barack Obama from a personal or professional fulfillment standpoint. They were mentors, and he welcomed their input as such.

In Figure 3, look carefully through the list of people President Obama handed responsibility to after achieving the executive office. You will see that he is quite a networker. He maintains relationships that extend from his law school days through the time of his work in the U.S. Senate (especially through Senator John Kerry and then-Senator Tom Daschle). In fact, five of Obama's insiders have connections to Kerry or Daschle:

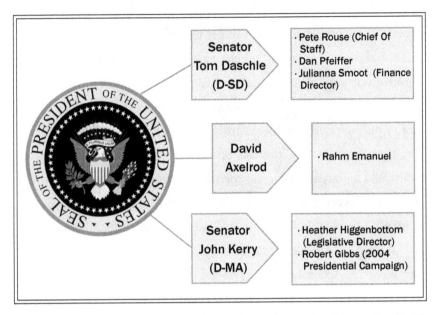

Figure 3: How the President Leveraged His Relational Capital and Network to Build His Team

Political chits, or credits, are earned and spent freely. However, the problem with many relationships, political and otherwise, is that people take capital and don't return it. As I mentioned earlier, balancing relationship capital is like a checkbook. You make withdrawals and you make deposits; you've still got to make sure there's always money in the account.

In a business setting, political capital is valued too. During my career, I've seen political capital used when people are competing for budgets or investment dollars, jockeying for the next promotion, being in the "inner circle," or moving business agendas forward.

AN ARMY EVERYWHERE IS AN ARMY NOWHERE

This quotation, a statement made by the Chinese military officer and philosopher Sun Tzu, applies to so many areas: management, leadership, military tactics, parenting, academics, research, and so forth. I interpret it to mean that focus is the key to success; you must pick your battles carefully and avoid being all things to all people.

The same applies for *effective* strategic networking. Networkers should be continually present in their network connections' hearts and minds even when, and maybe especially when, they are strategically absent. These connections are seeking a psychological presence. That's because a reputation is created or destroyed when the subject of that reputation is not physically present. As I mentioned earlier, *the selling happens when you are not around.*

Be selective about where you network and with whom. In addition, be aware that overexposure can happen if you don't manage your time effectively. People will believe that all you do is network if you spend most of your time attending events and being seen. Sometimes, less is more. When you pop up after an absence, you will realize (you hope) that you were missed and that people didn't take your presence for granted.

If you hear someone say about you, "He or she just meets people for a living," realize that it isn't a compliment. That's not the reputation you want. Don't join a network just to be in it: join with a goal or an outcome in mind. When I joined the Tower Club, for example, my only goal was to be around people who were in a different stratosphere than I was. I wanted to learn from them, and I wanted to see what successful people did. Since then, every time I've met somebody at the club, that's been because I wanted to be part of something he or she was doing, or I just wanted to help out.

As far as remaining in other people's networks, be very protective of your time. Make sure your activities align with your goals. Remember, too, that you shouldn't be introducing people into your network unless you know they meet your personal standards. Your reputation is on the line.

TREAD CAREFULLY

You may never have to use relational credits in your network, but knowing that you have the option to do so empowers you: it enables you to control your own destiny and manage your future.

This point is best illustrated by an anecdote. Once, I worked for a company that sold computer equipment to the government; specifically, the company sold to a government program office where I had worked in the past. The man running that government program office at the time happened to be a friend of mine.

The project didn't go well at all. Through a serious of missteps, including the system designers' lack of quality control, the prime contractor (a third party general contractor in charge of the project for which we supplied the equipment) blamed my company for all of the problems. As a result, he asked us to take the equipment back and return the millions of dollars his office had spent on the very high-end computing systems. However, because this project had been using the equipment for two years (and because my company had sold only the hardware and software, while having nothing to do with the system's design or overall project's engineering), I refused.

As you can imagine, we had plenty of blame to go around, and lots of finger pointing too. The government had problems with the prime contractor and the prime contractor had issues with the vendor, my company. My company was not at fault in this case because the problem was not with our hardware and software. Instead, the problem stemmed from the engineering and design methodologies the prime contractor was employing to build the system. In other words, the prime contractor's design concepts and plans couldn't fulfill the customer's expectations.

As the hardware and software vendor, my company was low on the totem pole. The prime contractor, who we worked for directly on this project, hammered us relentlessly, day and night, trying to make the case that the hardware was the problem. He called our CEO and as you can imagine, I received plenty of "help" from Corporate HQ. Finally, I decided to pull the equipment back in an effort to save the relationship. It cost our company money, our salespeople lost some of their commissions, and a general sense of ill will toward the prime contractor, based on how we were treated, developed.

About a year later, I ran into my friend—the guy who had been the government's program officer during that fiasco. He said, "You know, Sid, you could have just made a phone call and used your relationship with me to get past the whole mess, so that it didn't get ugly with your company."

I pointed out that these things happen on occasion and it's the cost of doing business. It wasn't the first time in history that somebody had not liked something they bought and wanted to return it, (although using the equipment for two years and wanting a full refund was a first). It happens.

He said, "But you could have called, and relied on the relationship. Yet you didn't. I really respect you for that."

I simply said, "Well it would have put you in a difficult situation since our contract was with the prime contractror and not with you. We tried to work with them, but were not successful."

He said, "Well, that's why you'll always have my business."

The lesson I learned from this experience is that we need to be very careful when using our relationship capital. While I could have leveraged my relationship with the customer (my friend), the project would have still been canceled in the end. Ultimately, we would have realized the same result (perhaps worse, if I had ridden the project to the end), while expending precious capital that had taken years to build. Instead, as a result of my approach, my connection and I were able to maintain a strong business and personal relationship for many years and our respective organizations could continue to partner down the road.

On the other hand, resolving business issues without pulling some strings isn't always possible. Many times, I've had to leverage personal relationships to get things done in business. For example, at one point my company had a very large contract about to come up for "re-compete." (When contracts end, the customer "re-competes" them: that is, the incumbent contractor may win or the contract may be awarded to a different contractor.) We had had this particular contract for over ten years and many companies wanted to take it away from us. Some employees of our competitors even went so far as to fabricate statements about how they would do a better job, saying that my company had become lazy after having the contract for so long. In the end, my personal relationship with the customer allowed my company to compete on a fair and level playing field. The customer trusted me and took my word as my bond; he listened when I presented what my company was prepared to do to ensure we were the best choice for him and his organization. In the end, we won the contract.

DO UNTO OTHERS

As I mentioned earlier, a network is made up of capital. It is capital to be invested, withdrawn, and valued. The network provides people with real, tangible benefits on multiple levels.

For example, recently I received an invitation to meet with four men with whom I was vaguely familiar. One was a CEO, while another was a former CEO. All of them were heavy hitters. I knew their names but I'd never had the pleasure of meeting them.

Soon after that initial meeting, I arranged to meet them individually for lunch and began developing a relationship with each. One, a former senior executive at a top technology company, asked me about my career, my current situation, and my background. We talked about people we knew in common and discussed the latest technology topics, including the emergence of cyber security.

I mentioned my position on the Board of Visitors of the National Defense University (NDU), saying that we had just published a new book, *Cyber Power and National Security*. I told him I'd be happy to have the author sign a copy and send it along. He said he'd be thrilled; he'd been trying to find a really good book on the subject.

So, I called NDU and asked that a signed copy of the book be sent to the executive. As you might imagine, he was delighted. To this day, we keep in touch. He has been a tremendous help to me as a mentor and as someone with whom I can bounce around ideas. He's also acted as a reference for me. However, in the end, he's become a friend, and that's the most important thing of all.

This small example illustrates the principle of reaching out to others in your network. What's the lesson here? Always look for opportunities to serve.

This gentleman didn't need anything from me. He didn't need my help at all. Since he was, and is, a wealthy, well-respected, and fine human being, you might be wondering, what could I possibly have had to offer him? You might be surprised. By paying attention, training my focus on him, and wondering what I might be able to do for him, I was able to come up with something that helped establish a connection. Had I been focused on myself, or on what he could do for me, I would have missed the opportunity to make that friendly gesture of sending him the book. As a result, our friendship might never have been.

When you reach out and expand your network, pay attention to what is interesting about or needed by others. People are often obsessed with and consumed by trying to get their own agendas accomplished; they forget the most effective solution is to help others achieve their own agendas. This is the ultimate "win-win."

Sometimes, people will tell me they don't have time for networking. My response is simple: Networking is what you do all day long, unless you work in total isolation. If you're in any industry—finance, engineering, government, marketing, technology, and so on—you're networking, or you have the opportunity to network. You are around people and you have the chance to meet others; that means the opportunities are there. Networking is an integral part of your business and your life. It's what you do, not something you have to make an extra effort to do.

There are, of course, networking opportunities that take place after work: you should make an extra effort to attend these dinners, events and social gatherings. However, most networking is done during the normal course of the day. Daily interaction becomes networking when you see it as networking, not just as casual interaction.

YES, THINGS GET DONE ON THE GOLF COURSE

Golf is a great way to get things done outside the office. It is a perfect networking pastime—perhaps the best in the business world. If you don't know how to play golf and you are in the business world,

I highly recommend you give it a try. While there are many activities that can provide the same networking opportunities as golf does, golf makes a great example for our purposes here.

I didn't start playing golf until I was thirty-four years old. I actually couldn't stand the game before I started playing. I'm a football player: why would I want to hit a little white ball with a stick? Then, one day, my boss said, "Let's play golf."

I had to admit to him that I didn't know how to play, which was a turning point for me. Soon after, I learned to play, and I'm glad I did: much gets done on the golf course. Playing golf gives you roughly five hours outdoors, away from the office, and in the fresh air. It's uninterrupted time with your foursome, especially your cart-mate. To benefit from golf, you don't have to play like Tiger Woods—you just have to play well enough to be respectable on the course.

When I was working at a large corporation, we had an annual officers' meeting. About 200 of us would fly out to Scottsdale, have three days of off-site meetings, and play a little golf. The big question on everyone's mind was always, "Who's going to play with the CEO?" One year, in particular, I knew I was being considered for a promotion. When I got the foursome list, I discovered that I was paired with the CEO. "Cool!" I thought. I'd met him before and he was a great guy.

Our foursome included a vice president, the general manager, the CEO, and me. When he heard the assignments, my boss called me in. He was a nervous wreck. "Don't do this, don't do that; don't say this, don't say that," he told me. He was chock full of alarmist advice.

I told him, "Thanks, I appreciate the advice and will let you know how things go with the CEO."

It turned out to be a very enjoyable round of golf; five hours of listening to him talk and interacting with the other people in my foursome. He got to know me and I got to know him.

I wound up getting the promotion, but not only because I played golf with the CEO. I got the promotion because I had the skills and network required for the job and became more known to him during our golf game. The golf game was sort of a final review to see if I could mesh with others and act appropriately in team settings. I've heard many stories about people who played golf with the boss hoping to get promoted, only to receive the opposite reaction. Largely, this would happen because of how they mishandled themselves on the golf course or because they inflated their abilities.

Think of it this way: how you handle yourself on the golf course can be indicative of how you handle yourself in other areas of your life. Golf reveals answers to the following questions:

- Do you stress out over the tough stuff?
- Do you exaggerate your prowess beforehand, only to be proved wrong?
- Do you use foul language when you miss something easy?
- Do you cheat just a little in order to get a better result?
- Do you get overly frustrated when you make bad calls or mistakes?
- Do you maintain decorum when you get frustrated?
- Finally, how do you interact with others?

Golf leads you through all the emotions of human nature. Whenever I play golf with other people, I always make sure I'm very controlled and measured. Always compliment an opponent who does well. "That was a great shot," I'll say: "You really got a hold of that one!" Even though it's a very individual sport, always try to be a team player. If someone slices the ball, I'm apt to point out something like, "The ball's probably flat on one side—it wasn't your fault." There are many dynamics going on out on the fairways, rough, traps, and greens.

When you play golf, you're being observed—sometimes even interviewed—but you don't know it. The interviewing is very subtle. I always advise people in the business world to "*Under promise and over deliver.*" That's especially true on the golf course. I've known people who bragged about being scratch golfers (in other words, those who shoot par), only to be teamed with a senior executive in the foursome. Senior executives are competitive and want to win. That's why they're senior executives! What ultimately happens in these situations, more often than not, is that the braggart is not a great golfer. The senior executive learns very quickly that the other person either isn't very self-aware, is full of hot air, or is just plain lying. All are bad traits to divulge at any time, much less during a five-hour round of golf. You're better off saying nothing, playing a respectable round, and coming out a hero.

Golf reveals other things too. For example, I've played golf with people who have made me very uncomfortable. Usually, that's because they manage to spoil the atmosphere of relaxed fun. Some people act like they're at an official PGA tournament, saying things like, "No, you can't take a mulligan!" or, "You've got to make the putt for it to count." The whole time, I'm thinking, "Gosh, we're not playing for money." It's very intense and, frankly, uncomfortable: certainly, it's not much fun when you're trying to relax.

People know that if they can spend five hours on a golf course with you and actually like you at the end of the day, then they can probably work with you, too. However, if they come out of the round thinking, "Wow, this guy has worn me out; he's just too intense," then you're not getting the job, the deal, the contract, or whatever else you may have hoped for as a result of the outing.

In short, people like golf because it's an excellent test. Golf reveals whether you can work well with others, and shows what your personality is like both when under stress and during good times. Are you a team player and a good sport? Have you got the kind of personality that enables people or saturates people? Golf will test your answers to those questions. That's why golf is important. If you really know how to play golf—by that, I mean not just playing the sport, but showing off your personality and managing the dynamics well—then you can emerge from the golf game in a very positive light.

EXPAND THE NETWORK

Always continue adding people to your network. In an open system like a network, order prevails. Once you make a new connection, your next thoughts should be: "Who's in this person's network? Is there something I can do for him or his network?" You also have to keep growing the network because some people are going to fall out over time. People get busy and lose touch, they move and lose touch, or they simply lose touch. In this age of ultra-connectivity, it behooves you to try and maintain all of your relationships, even though you won't be able to hold on to everyone. When that happens, don't be alarmed. Life goes on.

You can and should help others build their networks, but as you do so, make sure you are protected and expectations (both your own and others') are accurately set. Be willing to make introductions to other people, but don't allow yourself to be abused or spread too thin. Don't damage your reputation for the sake of other people. Define your network by the center, not by the margins.

Finally, remember that network capital is real capital: it can be accumulated and spent just like gold or other currency. It can be leveraged in the same way that money can be leveraged. So, use it wisely, and don't let your supply lines reach the breaking point. Likewise, be present in the hearts and minds of your network. Delight others: outdo them in kindness and generosity. Grow the network, and learn to play golf!

TAKEAWAYS FROM CHAPTER SIX

- The network has various forms of capital, all of which provide value.
- Network capital should be spent carefully.
- You must win hearts and minds of the network.
- t
- Identify activities in which you can spend time with others, so you facilitate network building.
- Golf can play a key role in developing (or destroying) business relationships.

THE ART OF NETWORK OPERATIONS

CHAPTER 7

"And in the end, the love you take is equal to the love you make."
—*The Beatles*

Maintaining and effectively operating your network is perhaps the most important thing you can do in order both to preserve your sanity and further growth and development. It's also one of the hardest things you can do. Until I started creating my network, I didn't realize how much effort it takes. In other words, when I first started networking, I was naïve. I had watched my father do it, but he was a natural. He made networking look easy: he had no hesitation or apprehension about meeting and talking with people he didn't know. Keeping things moving and keeping the network alive takes a lot of energy.

STAY ON THE RADAR

The first thing to keep in mind when networking, is that you need to *stay on the radar*. You do this most effectively by, for example, attending events where you can meet with your network, sending an occasional email message, holding a lunch or dinner meeting, making phone calls, and mailing holiday or birthday cards. (As I mentioned earlier, writing handwritten notes can be a boost to your networking efforts.) Staying in touch is so much easier today than it was even thirty years ago. With a Blackberry or Smart Phone, you can talk to anyone in the world. When you send an email or a text, the recipient has it seconds later. There is absolutely no reason—there is no excuse—for not staying connected to people.

Another way to stay on the radar is to forward an interesting article you came across to a few select people who will find it relevant. When you read something fascinating, try to think who else is likely to find it interesting. Of the maybe twenty people I haven't been in touch with for a long time, perhaps three of them would find it relevant and to their taste. If I find an article about the New Orleans Saints, I'll send it to all of my New Orleans buddies. If I find an article about music or guitars, I'll send it to my musician friends. If I locate an article about the CIA, I will send it to my CIA buddies. If I locate an article about motorcycles, I will send it to my motorcycle buddies. Even though I've got all these different networks, I stay on top of them with techniques like this one. It really doesn't take much time at all.

When you apply this technique, forward the article with a message along the lines of: "I read this article and thought you would find it interesting. Enjoy! Hope you're doing well." You'll soon learn that the usual response is something like, "Great to hear from you! When are we going to get together?" The interaction takes off on its own and you don't have to work at it.

While it can be challenging, it's important to find opportunities to do more than grab lunch with members of your network. You have to find something that maintains your interest and connection. For example, I have several close friends whom I might not see for several months, but we work to stay in touch, and we connect eventually.

Keep cycling through time with your friends. You might ask, "Well, how do you get any work done if you spend all your time keeping in touch with people?" I'm not talking about reaching out for twenty or thirty hours a week. What does it cost you, in terms of time, to have lunch or breakfast with someone once or twice a week? *Effective networkers will find ways to integrate their network connections into their daily activities*, whether through golf, travel, or events, and so forth. Like anything else worth having, you have to work at maintaining your connections.

People have to see you in action. You have to be out and be visible. For example, I usually go to a popular local diner for breakfast. I know I'll run into several colleagues there, which is precisely what I want. Breakfast meetings work well because they take place first thing in the morning. You can knock them out quickly and get to work. Regardless of where you go, however, you've got to put yourself out there. People have to see you. If you're not present, they'll forget about you. You could be the CEO of a company, but if people don't hear from you, see you, or read about you, then they will forget you exist. As one executive said to me, "*Out of sight, out of mind, out of business.*" You have to stay on the radar.

PHONE AND EMAIL ETIQUETTE

Don't pester people. If you leave a voicemail or send an email and don't receive a response, wait a few days. It could be that the recipient is out of town or just swamped. My general rule is if I contact someone and don't hear back within two to three days, I'll reach out once more to say, "Just want to be sure you got my message."

One of the most irritating things you can do is call someone and leave a message that you need to talk urgently, when you truly do not. Then, when that person responds immediately and you don't respond in turn, but instead wait three or four more days before responding, that's bad form. Good phone and email etiquette is extremely important for maintaining strong relationships. I simply don't believe it when people say they were too busy to return a phone call or an email. This is one of my biggest pet peeves. If someone in your network calls you or sends an email, respond as soon as you can, even if just to say, "I'm really busy at the moment. Can I get back to you?" Being too busy to return an email or a phone call is a poor excuse and everyone knows it. Besides, everyone is busy these days! Don't be known as someone who doesn't return phone calls or emails. That's just not acceptable. When people use the excuse that they are too busy to respond to me, I interpret this as rudeness or ineffective time management. Both are career and relationship killers.

Networking takes time. So, don't network with people who don't manage their networking time, or yours, responsibly. This is something of which you have to be continuously aware.

If somebody's not respectful or lacks a basic understanding of your time constraints, that can be a turn-off. Maintain your situational and emotional awareness. Realize that if you are talking with someone who has to meet and speak with many people at a large event, your time with him or her is limited.

Remember, as I discussed earlier, *the objective in the first meeting is to get a second meeting.* That's why you should ask for a business card. Get the other person's contact information. Let a day or two go by. Then, reach out with a simple message, such as, "It was great meeting you the other night. I'd like to meet for lunch to continue our discussion. Let me know when you're free." This process is slightly similar to dating. If you chase the other party too hard, he or she will avoid you. That's human nature. If you don't hear back from someone, take it as a sign: the other person might not have the same level of interest in pursuing the relationship that you do.

Just as you are required to respect other people's time when you're meeting or getting to know them, you have to budget your own networking time. Another earlier rule bears repeating: *An army everywhere is an army nowhere.* If you're not surgical in your approach to networking, you can spread yourself too thin.

Another tactic that can kill relationships is using a secretary or executive assistant (EA) to reach out to the person with whom you want to build a relationship. When you are building a relationship—and, even more importantly, when you have built and are maintaining the relationship—never treat that relationship as pedestrian. I've experienced this on more than one occasion. In fact, it's happened both with people I've known for twenty years and with people who are in the process of trying to build a relationship with me. These people have their EA make an initial contact to schedule a meeting. The EA calls and says, "Mr. Fuchs, please hold for Mr. X." In such circumstances, I politely hang up the phone.

If a relationship is important to you, then take the extra ten seconds to dial the phone yourself. Get someone on the line or send a quick email to make the connection personally. There is nothing wrong with asking your EA to follow up and do the coordination, but the first contact to request a meeting or a phone conversation should come from you. Nothing says disrespect and egotism more than having someone else dial your phone or send an email on your behalf.

STRATEGIC ABSENCE

As I mentioned earlier, strategic absence and silence have power. Sometimes, silence is truly golden. It can effectively get people's attention. So, don't saturate the market with yourself. It can pay to be a little aloof. If people are used to you pinging them on a regular basis, hearing from you loses its specialness. These people may stop responding. At that point, the clever thing is to quit pinging them. They'll come back to you and say, "I haven't heard from you in a while."

You then respond with, "Yes, well, I was emailing you and you didn't respond, so I figured you were busy and I didn't want to bother you." How you respond in such a situation goes back to knowing how people like to respond to things.

ALLOW OTHERS THE CHANCE TO HELP

People like to feel needed; they like to be asked for help. So, ask for advice. The best way to get involved in a network is to ask questions: "What do you think? How would you do this? What do you recommend?" Asking for advice or help is a powerful way to handle things.

Next, put yourself in a position that encourages people to want to help. I could count on one hand the number of times I have overtly asked for something from my network. Usually, the network will provide something of value without my having to ask. When real relationships form, it is natural for both parties to want to help each other. Once people in the network start offering to help you, they genuinely like you, and they know what your objectives are, you are achieving mutual value. That's a real network.

NEVER CONFUSE POSITION WITH RELEVANCE

Networks can be sustained over time if people want to know you, versus if they *have* to know you because of your position. Some people in the world are networked because of the titles and positions they hold. It doesn't mean others like them; it means people know them *because it's required.* You can tell how plugged in these people are after they leave their positions. Do they still have the same network connections? To sustain a long-lasting network, people have to want to know you because of who you are, not what you do. *Your position may get you the initial contact, but who you are will help you grow and sustain your relationship with that contact.*

The above is an important thing to recognize. Some people enjoy the perks of their positions without ever investing in relationships, which they take for granted too often. Once they lose their positions or prominence—by resigning, getting fired, or retiring—they lose their relevance. Then, they feel like they've lost their value. However, you don't have to lose your relevance if you've created genuine relationships. I've worked in several companies over the past twenty-five years, and with every move, my network has grown exponentially.

THE IMPORTANCE OF FRIENDSHIP

Networking works best across the board when you can use it to nurture genuine friendships. One proverb, "A friend in need is a friend indeed," sums up a strong network. You must always be there for your friend. You must always do what you can for someone in your network; that's part of the reason you need to be selective about who you bring into that network. You must be strategic. You want people who will watch your back as you watch theirs. As Aristotle said, "A friend to all is a friend to none." There is a lot of truth in that observation. The more you spread yourself thin, the less likely it is you will be able to be there for a friend in need. There's just nothing left to give.

It's always easier to be there for people you like—for people you identify with and enjoy spending time with. It makes sense that people prefer to do business with people they like. Why would you get involved in spending time with people you don't particularly like, or worse yet, people you don't particularly trust? This goes back to one of my book's initial premises: *Trust is the currency of all relationships.* It's very difficult to trust people with whom you don't have a natural affinity.

COMMUNICATE, COMMUNICATE, COMMUNICATE

Everyone knows that communication is perhaps the most important skill in human relations. Yet it remains a huge challenge for many people. Some people believe they have the magic bullet for effective communication. They have saturated the human interaction field with their expertise on topics like marriage, friendship, business communication, platform skills, preaching, negotiation skills, and persuasion, as well as all manner of general psychology.

I won't add to the already extensive literature on the subject. Not only would it be presumptuous of me, but even if I had some shining gem, it would get lost in the already glittering pile. All I can say, with authority, is that communication matters. It matters a lot. So, make the effort to communicate with your network. You don't need to communicate too much (remember the idea of strategic absence, or silence), but, as a general rule, it is better to err on the side of too much communication, not too little. Obviously, the best type of communication is in person, but when that can't take place, electronic and phone communications also work.

Communication within the network is not about "selling" yourself, or convincing others you are worthy. All too often, we try to sell our value when we don't need to do so. Discussions within a network are genuine; they are based on common interests, goals, and ways to help and get to know others. If you're not having these conversations, then you're not in a true network.

UNDERSTANDING PROTOCOLS

A communications protocol is a set of standard rules for data representation, signaling, authentication, and error detection that is required for sending information over a communications channel. Computer networks use communication protocols, and so do human networks. You should understand how people in your network like to communicate. If you don't understand communication protocols, you might be easily offended or you might easily offend someone.

For example, I have a friend who simply doesn't respond to an email unless I specifically ask him to do so. For example, I'll send him an email saying, "It was great to see you this morning. Thanks for breakfast." In response, I'll get nothing. Silence. However, if I send him an email saying, "I'm sending you a link—would you mind telling me what you think?," then he'll respond immediately. If I didn't understand his protocol, I might find his silence somewhat off-putting, but it's just how he is. If I were ever to ask him for anything, I have no doubt he'd move heaven and earth to oblige me. So, I think it's important to understand everyone's communication styles—their communication protocols, if you will—and how they prefer to interact. The way I deal with this friend is different than the way I deal with other people.

At the onset of a relationship, reveal yourself, but don't be judgmental. If you and I meet at a party, you might say, "I work at XYZ, Inc."

In response, I might say, "Oh, really? Do you know Joe Smith? Man, what a great guy."

Well, *you* may not like the guy at all for reasons known only to you. At that point, because I've sung the praises of your archenemy, you may not want to know me. This goes back to knowing your audience. When meeting somebody for the first time, don't have a judgmental or opinionated discussion. Give perspectives: don't make declarations. The point is that it's better to learn about and assess the other person before you start making declarative judgments. Remember, *reading the situation is a key skill in developing your network.*

A safe way to act during your first meeting is to ask questions about or of the other person. With this approach, you learn more about the other person and start to understand sensitive areas and land mines, as well as what is interesting about him or her.

For instance, one night in 1995, just after the Oklahoma City bombing, I was at a business function. A few of my colleagues and many law enforcement officers and officials also attended. One of the guys who happened to work for me came up to a small group, including some of those law enforcement professionals. He commented that the function was boring; perhaps someone should blow up the building to get some excitement going.

The law enforcement officers in the group had lost friends in the recent Oklahoma City bombing, so you can imagine what their reaction was. They all turned around and walked away from the group.

I asked my colleague, "Do you know who we were talking to? Those guys just lost friends in the bombing, and you're talking about blowing up a building?" After that conversation, it was hard to get our company back in good graces with law enforcement officials for a long time. They took that careless comment very personally, as they should have, and as anybody would.

THE IMPORTANCE OF LOYALTY

Be loyal and inspire trust. This is something that we don't always do. I've been guilty of it as well. When you meet somebody for the first time and start talking about people you know in common, sometimes loose comments are made. I'm talking about the occasional impulsive remark, like "Yeah, I know so-and-so. He's wacko—in fact, the guy's certifiable. I don't understand how he's successful." Once someone has said that, the first thing the new acquaintance is going to wonder is: *Will he say things like that about me when I'm not around?*

It's better to say something like, "Well, so-and-so is a good guy—a little different, but a good guy," and leave it at that. You don't want to overcorrect and say, "Yeah, so-and-so is phenomenal; he's the greatest thing." Then, the new acquaintance may wonder whether the speaker is out of touch with reality. This means you've got to be very balanced, but you've also got to be loyal. You can't disrespect people because then they won't respect you; moreover, they'll wonder whether you're a back-stabber, which is a bad type of reputation to have.

The art of network maintenance is also the art of human relations. Both are about strategic and surgical communication; they are about friendship, fellowship, and good fun. The network needs to be nurtured, especially when you think you don't need it. The time may come when you do need it and you want it to be there for you. To that end, you want to have friends you can rely on and be connected to people who will watch your back. To get that, you need to be there for them when they need you and you need to watch their backs. This all comes down to loyalty, integrity, and respect. Make no mistake: as I keep reiterating, *trust is the currency of all relationships.*

TAKEAWAYS FROM CHAPTER SEVEN

- A network must be maintained and requires effort.
- Maintain visibility without oversaturating the network.
- Discover strategic absence and learn how to make people miss you.
- Be a friend and give people what they want and need.
- Maintain lines of communications and find ways to connect.
- Be loyal: inspire trust and confidence.
- Learn to read the situation and the other person before you reveal your position or opinions.

THE NETWORK IS FOR EVERYONE

CHAPTER 8

"Solitude is fine, but you need someone to tell you that solitude is fine."
—*Honoré de Balzac*

We have talked about the art of networking, about planning your network, and about how to leverage it. Still, some folks resist networking because they think their personality or style isn't conducive to the process. The good news is that this point is not true. Networking is for *everyone*, regardless of people's personalities, styles, or preferences.

Let's start with a discussion of how different types of people network. We all have personality, style, and charm. Yes, we all do. We can think of a person in terms of an extrovert vs. an introvert (that is, someone who is outgoing vs. shy). For that matter, we may consider the type-A personality (someone who has excessive competitiveness and ambition, an obsession with accomplishing tasks quickly, little time for self-reflection, and a strong need to control situations) and the type-B personality (someone who is relaxed, not competitive, and inclined to self-analysis).

However, let's not get bogged down by personality types. There is no "right" personality for networking. Networking may come more easily or naturally to an extrovert, but it need not take an introvert too far out of his or her comfort zone. As we'll see shortly, introverts just have a different style of networking. I think it is important to point out that the more social adeptness skills you have, the better your chances of creating and maintaining a network.

IS ANYONE EXCLUDED FROM NETWORKING?

Some people may still ask, "Is networking an exclusive pastime for certain types of people?" The answer is an emphatic "No!" Indeed, relationships are vital to the human condition. We cannot live without them—at least, not for long.

I remember attending one event and hearing a guest speaker talking to a fairly intimate gathering about the importance of fellowship. Early in his address, when he was standing in front of a roaring fire, he took a pair of tongs, removed a large and flaming log from the fire, and set it several feet away on the hearth. It was not long before the log lost its flame and began smoldering. It eventually went cold. He was able to pick it up with his bare hands and place it back in the fire, where it immediately burst into flames again. He never said a word about it, but the point was beautifully made: Left to our own devices, we grow cold and die.

CHARISMA, PASSION AND GROWING TALLER

Charisma is not an inherent quality one is born with, but instead, is a learned behavior. The simplest way to be an appealing person is to find others fascinating and to genuinely be interested in them. We all love to be loved, and we find those who love us appealing. Look people in the eye and listen to them intently. Really listen, don't just pretend to listen. Find people fascinating and they will remember it—and you.

I'll tell you a little secret about snake charming. Snakes are easily charmed. Sit in front of a closed basket with a cobra inside (preferably an Indian cobra), and play a flute, swaying the instrument back and forth. Summon your magical powers for the crowd that will inevitably form. Appear to be in a trance. Then, lift the lid of the basket, still playing the music and swaying your flute. The cobra will rise from the basket, flare its hood, and begin swaying back and forth. Easy, right?

Note: Snakes are deaf. They are not swaying to the music—they sway naturally. They rise from their baskets because they prefer light to darkness. So, if you're charming a snake, just be sure to sit back, out of biting range!

The moral of the story is this: Allow people to do what comes naturally to them and they will love you for it. The world will believe you to be charismatic and charming. The benefit is that you will in fact be charming, for perception in human relations is reality. If you can create an environment in which people can relax, be themselves, and not feel threatened or on guard, then you will be someone people want to be around. Make people feel easy (not defensive), and watch your network, as well as your inclusion in other networks, expand.

Remember that passion, like selfless love, is a matter of choice. The ancient Greeks recognized four types of love: *storge* (natural love that cannot be avoided—that of a mother for her child or a child for ice cream); *philos* (brotherly love or love for a friend); *eros* (chemical love that also cannot be avoided, characterized by butterflies in the stomach and weakness of the knees); and *agape* (selfless love that is entirely by choice).

Passion has some of the same characteristics. There are natural passions (formed by nature and nurture, such as political and social causes) and there are chosen passions (such as hang-gliding, lead toy soldier collecting, and hunting). Networking falls into the latter categories of both love and passion. It is chosen. You may by nature and nurture be more or less inclined to network. However, to actually network, you must make the choice to be passionate about it.

Of course, there are still some things you have no control over. It is no good if a basketball coach tells his players to grow taller. While it's true that they might be better at basketball if they were taller, the suggestion just doesn't help them. They can't simply decide to grow taller.

In the same vein, I will not tell you to be more outgoing. It might be easier for you to network if you were more outgoing, but becoming more outgoing may be too much to ask of you, based on your particular DNA. Instead, I suggest that you work within your personality's strengths and figure out what works best for you. There are many areas in which you can excel that don't require an outgoing personality. Returning to the basketball analogy, you can be a great scorer (especially of three-pointers), passer, team player, and clutch performer without being notably tall. Similarly, in networking you can be a great note taker, sincere listener, be honest and trustworthy, be a great friend, and bring a lot to the table, all without being particularly outgoing.

INTROVERTS AND PRE-ESTABLISHED COMMON GROUND

An introvert will typically want to meet other people on common ground. That is, an introvert may prefer a small wine tasting to a more traditional networking event. At a wine tasting, you can be pretty sure that everybody present likes wine. So, there is always at least one thing to talk about that's not the weather (most introverts despise small talk). The same thing goes for a church picnic (although perhaps such an event has a bit less certainty of common ground) or an art opening. All this is not to say that introverts are more cultured than extroverts (who may of course attend the same functions); instead, I suggest that introverts may be more comfortable at small gatherings, which present very definite common ground, than they would be at, say, the Kentucky Derby, a pub crawl, or a club meet-and-greet.

An introvert may tend to seek commonality because it's safe; it requires less skill or effort than meeting someone you don't know in unchartered territory does. My wife, an introvert, agrees with this point absolutely. If she doesn't know anybody at an event, or has no reason to be somewhere, she is a bit uncomfortable. However, when she went to a cooking class with another friend (who's also an introvert), they met lots of people. They were completely at ease because everyone in the group had a common interest.

In contrast, if I (the extrovert) met you at a wine tasting, we would talk about the wine for about thirty seconds before I couldn't stand it any longer and started to ask about you, "Where do you live? What do you do for fun? Do you play golf? Do you ride motorcycles? What do you like?" For me, it's all about you and finding the connection.

Meanwhile, at the same event, the introverts are probably discussing wine: "What do you think of this or that wine? What kind of wine do you serve with a big steak? Do you like to cook with wine? Where do you store it? Do you have a cellar at home?" Such conversation is comfortable and it gets the job done. As people get comfortable chatting with each other, they begin to get to know each other. So, introverts can network just as effectively; their methods are just a little different.

EXTROVERTS AND CREATING COMMON GROUND ON THE FLY

One thing I've noticed about extroverts is that they have to be careful when connecting with introverts. It's helpful to be aware of this if you're an extrovert who's trying to connect with someone who happens to be an introvert. If someone is quiet and reserved, you need to take a reserved approach when you meet him or her. Sit back and observe people for a while, to determine their style, before you approach them. Be cognizant of the people that you're trying to connect with. Remember, even when extroverts dial back their energy and style, they are still often seen as extroverts. As I mentioned before, while you can't change who or what you are, you can certainly modulate your style to fit the situation.

Both introverts and extroverts have to be aware of the type of person they're approaching. You have to make sure you're on the same frequency with the new contact. When I'm dealing with people who are very reserved, or very quiet, I find myself toning down, naturally. After many years of practice, I can speak in a much more reserved, calm, and slow-paced voice. I've got a friend, a recruiter, who talks really fast. When we talk to each other we both talk really fast, and we're all set. We like each other, but for our communication to succeed, it's important that I mirror his style.

YOUR PREFERRED APPROACH TO NETWORKING

You can't use introversion as an excuse for not networking. Introversion means you may use a different sort of networking based on pre-arranged common ground. The principles and techniques of networking still apply. You simply need to modify your approach and style in a way that is appropriate for the situation at hand. That caution goes for everybody. You shouldn't network in an unnatural way, because then you won't be yourself, and the networking will become hard. Instead, you've got to find a style and approach that works best for you.

Introversion and extroversion are useful descriptions for how people recharge their batteries or interact, but they do not predetermine networking proficiency. You simply have to figure out the networking style that works best for you and begin practicing it. Remember that practice builds skill, skill builds self-confidence, and self-confidence leads to more networking.

So be charming, be passionate, and go forth and prosper!

TAKEAWAYS FROM CHAPTER EIGHT

- ◦ Introverts are not at a disadvantage when it comes to networking. If you're an introvert, find a common ground with your contact.
- ◦ Differing personality styles and traits require you to modify your approach to networking, not to change your personality, which you cannot do.
- ◦ Charm and passion always make for good form.
- ◦ Introverts search for common ground or interests through which to network, while extroverts create common ground through which to network.

SOCIAL MEDIA NETWORKS

CHAPTER 9

"Focus on how to be social, not on how to do social."
—*Jay Baer*

What is a social media network? Let's define it as an Internet site where people can share information and ideas, join groups of mutual interest, and promote their businesses using viral marketing techniques.

Social media networks are auxiliary tools, not primary tools, used to network. Never replace live, personal communication with texting, Internet usage, or email. Just because somebody's one of your connections on Facebook or LinkedIn doesn't necessarily mean that person is in your physical network. He or she may be in your network, technically, but only in your virtual network.

At present, I have over 1,400 connections on LinkedIn. Many of these connections are what I would call casual acquaintances. I may have met these people, but don't have any real history or experience with them. Still, I'll always connect to people—that's just how I am. However, once we're connected, that doesn't mean I know these people well enough to write them a recommendation. Our relationship does not exist in actuality. So, it is critical to distinguish between virtual networking and personal networking; they are two different things.

Just because people are connected to other folks on a portal or one of the social media pages doesn't mean they're in a strategic network. They may be in a virtual network, but that doesn't mean that they can necessarily leverage their contacts to get value out of the relationship. Remember, when forming a network, you always have to look at whether or not there is a way to extract value from or provide value to a relationship.

If I don't know a social media contact personally—if I haven't vetted that person or done a background check—I'm not going to introduce that person to my network as though I do know him or her. That's not to say this individual will never become part of my network. If I were to strike up a correspondence with a "stranger" to whom I am connected in my social or virtual network, we would eventually be able to meet, at least by phone. Certainly, it's possible to become real friends, in the real world, with formerly virtual contacts.

Years from now, there may be thirty-year-olds in office cubicles who cannot conceive of personal networks that aren't just subsets of whatever networks they formed on Facebook while growing up. Yet virtual networking does not, nor will it ever, replace personal networking, because it removes the human element. If you don't have the human element, there's no way networking can be truly effective.

REMEMBER, IT'S JUST A TOOL: NEVER CUT WOOD WITH A HAMMER

Even though I am generally not regarded as an early adopter of new technology, I am the first to admit the value in something new, like social media. However, we need to be careful, and we must consider social networking as a tool in the toolkit of human relations. Social networking is a novel and exciting way to connect with people (who have similar interests) from across the globe. That's really cool.

There are hundreds of websites dedicated to connecting people. For our purposes, let's look at just a few of the sites—the ones used by businesses. Significantly, some of the top business sites also happen to be top social sites. Facebook and LinkedIn are at some of the highest points on both lists. Both have broad applications for the social networking scene.

Facebook was started strictly for college students, accessible by invitation only. Now the whole world uses it. As of this writing, there are some 750 million active Facebook users at last count. Facebook can be an effective tool if it's used properly. I see more and more senior people—those in their sixties and seventies—getting on Facebook. I asked one of them why and he said, "Everyone else is on it!" By using Facebook, I've reconnected with people I haven't seen in years, so there's certainly value to it.

LinkedIn, the business-networking site, is a valuable tool that can indicate what is occurring in the industry. For example, if I get an abnormally high number of hits on my LinkedIn profile over a short period of time, all from people in the same company, then I can ascertain that the company has layoffs ahead. People are looking to see who can help them navigate through potential layoffs. The same goes for executive recruiters; if they are accessing my profile that means someone is looking at me for a position.

I've been on LinkedIn for several years and have never received a single spam message through it. I did, however, recently have an experience that made me a little uncomfortable. A couple of weeks ago, one of my LinkedIn contacts sent me an email introducing me to a third party. She didn't send it through the usual, acceptable LinkedIn channels, and I felt awkward about it. (By the way, you should always ask someone if they want to be introduced to a third person before you actually make the introduction. The answer might be, "No, not right now.") Still, I responded to the person I didn't know, saying, "Hey, nice to meet you," and so on. I eventually told my friend in a very nice way that it would be helpful to me if she could discuss introductions with me before she made them in the future. She understood my concerns and now we have a good understanding of how to network with each other.

I didn't know who he was, and I had nothing in common with him, but my LinkedIn contact thought we might like each other because we were both from Louisiana and had ended up in the Washington, D.C. area for decades. That was it.

At that point, I felt a little violated. I don't like people making third-party introductions unless they clear it with me first. When you're in somebody else's network, you shouldn't do that either. Instead, feel free to say to someone, "I have a person who you might like to meet. Here's who he is and his background; are you interested?" The person may say, "Maybe later, but not right now; I'm pretty busy," "No, thanks, I'm good," or, "Absolutely, set it up!"

Another friend of mine used to spontaneously email me introductions to his friends because he thought we needed to know each other. Quickly, I asked him to stop doing that and to check with me before he made introductions. Remember, as the network owner, you should always reserve the right to determine with whom you are and aren't connected. If other people start making introductions without your approval, you should follow up. Do not ignore the email introduction, because you are a courteous professional. If you don't limit these outside introductions, though, you could lose control of your network and how you invest your time in new relationships. Be protective of your time.

UNDER SURVEILLANCE AND OVEREXPOSED

We are under constant watch each day: cell phone cameras, traffic cameras, and security cameras all capture us. It is amazing to watch the news and see how almost any event can be captured on video or in photos. Remember when actor Michael Richards (Kramer from *Seinfeld*) starting ranting racial slurs in a nightclub, back in 2006? His behavior was captured on someone's cell phone and the cell video made the talk-show circuit. Needless to say, his reputation was impacted by his actions, which the whole world was able to see first-hand. He retired from stand-up comedy in 2007, and I am sure his actions in 2006 accelerated his retirement. So, as I always tell my children, be good or end up on YouTube!

Sites like Facebook, LinkedIn, and Twitter allow you to connect with people who know you personally and who you don't really know at all. The site isn't a real network in the sense of a value-added network and I think people get overexposed by using it at times. I find it humorous when Facebook or Twitter users operate on the assumption that I am, or anybody else is, interested in their mundane, daily routine: "I woke up, I had breakfast, and now I'm going to the mall…" People get overexposed. This overexposure takes the mystery out of who you are and what you're about. If there's one rule of thumb, especially in the business world, it's this: You want to have a little mystery surrounding you. If everybody knows everything about you, you're not interesting anymore.

Speaking of the need to be discrete and vigilant about exposing yourself on social networks, a friend who leases high-end corporate apartments told me an interesting story. One of his salespeople posted a photo of a fairly rollicking party on Facebook. Unfortunately, the picture clearly showed that the party had taken place in one of the beautifully appointed, new corporate apartments. The salesperson obviously had a key to the apartment, which had not yet been leased. The incident almost cost him his job. Fortunately for him, my friend showed mercy: the guy was a good salesperson who was unlikely to pull a stunt like that again. Besides, he told me, the old adage is true: "There's no law against stupidity."

NOTHING BEATS MANO-A-MANO HUMAN INTERACTION

Let me reiterate this point: there is no substitute for good, old-fashioned, face-to-face time. Email, text messaging, and social networking are fine for pinging friends and staying on people's radar. However, you cannot sustain a meaningful relationship in 140-character bursts.

My teenage sons, like all teenagers in today's world, use texting and email as their primary form of communication. This doesn't really impact them when they are in their peer groups, since all their peers communicate the same way, too. What I have noticed, however, is that teenagers today, for the most part, don't have very developed *live* communication skills. Usually, but not always, when I ask my sons or their friends how things are going, or when I try to engage them in conversation, I can sometimes get a one-word answer or a grunt. This means I have to work harder if I want to have a conversation.

On more than a few occasions, I have had to coach my sons on acceptable communication expectations. These are valuable skills to teach your teenagers as they mature, so that eventually, they can enter the workforce. Realize, though, that this is not their fault—this is the way of the world for their generation. Teenagers are more comfortable in their own age group, but not as comfortable with outside age groups. While this may have always been true of teenagers, I believe the overuse of electronic communication is stunting our youth's desire and ability to express their thoughts verbally.

In days gone by, people managed to sustain long-distance relationships by post; they wrote long, imaginative, and thoughtful letters. Unfortunately, letter writing is a dying art because of instant communication. Because we have social networks, people can update their life stories on a moment-by-moment basis. Of course, this begs the question: how do you live your life if you spend it posting updates to your Facebook profile? (Such behavior also negates the need for philosophical inquiry and self-reflection, but that is not the subject of this book.)

Suffice it to say that we are social creatures. Our lives ought to be shared, but not on a momentary basis. We are not open books. The Millennial generation does not seem to recognize a fundamental right to—or desire for—privacy. I don't get it, but there we are.

And yet . . . having said all that, we have to adapt to these social networks; we have to catch the wave of the future. People who aren't on Facebook, LinkedIn, or Twitter are going to miss something important as the world continues to connect and evolve.

Even so, we have to realize that there's not much "stickiness" to most of these virtual relationships fostered on social networking sites. "Stickiness" refers to when you provide and receive value in a long-term relationship. Social media is important, but it can get you in trouble or overexpose you. While you do need to be very careful with it, you also need to be able to embrace it. That's because it's here to stay: you're not going to be able to get away from it.

Now, a whole generation spends more time texting and checking their Facebook and Twitter networks than engaging in almost any other category of behavior. A cottage industry of university studies on technology addiction is growing across the nation. The results of these studies are astonishing: we are dealing with a generation of technology junkies. At this point, the long-term impacts of social media networks are hard to imagine. I won't make any predictions, other than to suggest that new branches of psychology and law will be created in order to deal with the effects of being simultaneously connected and disconnected.

TAKEAWAYS FROM CHAPTER NINE

- o You cannot avoid social media networks.
- o These networks have their place among the spectrum of networking tools and techniques.
- o Don't confuse real or physical networks with virtual networks.
- o Remember, real networks are built on real relationships.
- o What you say or do online or offline can be posted online, so be careful.
- o Nothing replaces face-to-face interaction.

EPILOGUE

It is hard to argue that having friends, supporters, or partnerships could ever be a bad thing. Sure, gaining these connections takes time, patience, and resources, as well as the desire to connect. What I learned along the way is that I get more joy out of helping others than I do from having someone help me. When I woke up one day and started taking an inventory all of the people in my life that I've been able to help—whether I made small or significant contributions—I realized that helping others is what life's about.

I hope this book has made you aware of some new concepts, techniques, and perspectives about strategic networking. Some of the points may be obvious, but that's what makes networking accessible to and available for everyone. My goal in this book has been to take you through my networking experiences, to show you what worked and didn't work for me, and to reveal how I managed to make my way through these efforts. I can honestly say that I owe much of what I've been able to accomplish in my life to my network—including my friends and family—from my childhood to today. No one (and I do mean no one) does it alone. We all have and need support throughout our lives. This book's mission is to help you see that you can create a network that will provide you with the aid you may need to receive, or the assistance you may need to give, as you go through life's journey.

Just as when you buy a new car and suddenly start noticing the number of people driving a car like yours, now I hope that you will notice when "networking" is taking place and how it plays a role because you have been introduced to various views about, perspectives on, techniques for, and stories of networking . The more you see networking, the more you will appreciate it, and the more you will develop your own style and techniques that work best for you.

No one gets networking right all the time, but perseverance pays off. After all, just like in baseball, you can't hit a home run unless you take a swing at the ball. So, *get off the bench*, step up to the plate, take a swing, and see where it takes you. The people you meet just may pleasantly surprise you.

APPENDIX A

MENTOR CAPITAL: GROWING A COMPANY'S MOST PRECIOUS RESOURCE

Sidney E. Fuchs

15 April 2002

Why is mentoring important for an organization's future? Who should be a mentor, and what does that require? This article examines these and other issues.

Mentors can provide a number of valuable functions within any business group: a mentor can be a role model, teacher, listener, coach, and all-around supporter. Mentoring can also assume many different forms, but, fundamentally, a mentor's job is to enable others by sharing experience and knowledge. It is widely acknowledged that an organization's ability to mentor or coach others is a corporate asset, so, logically, we would expect most companies to make teaching others an integral part of their corporate culture. If they invest working capital (cash, for example) to maximize the company's worth and help drive their business, why wouldn't they do the same with their people?

Unfortunately, too often organizations either overlook or just plain ignore this critical aspect of corporate investment, which is a huge mistake. In fact, some organizations promote the opposite of mentoring. By placing too much emphasis on looking good in front of the boss, as well as making constant demands of employees to prove themselves (in order to preserve their jobs), these companies encourage people to hoard information and skills so others can't "steal" them. This is shortsighted. Without "mentor capital," an organization has a dim future. The reasons for this are quite simple. Unless everyone is on the same page, executing against the same goals and taking responsibility for their actions, teams can quickly become fragmented and internally focused. This is a characteristic of a low-trust environment in which people feel the need to protect and preserve their own interests above those of the team.

Mentor capital is especially crucial for software development organizations because they typically cannot take advantage of "economies of scale." Most software projects, in fact, suffer from a "diseconomy of scale," which means they can't achieve improvement (in performance, quality, schedule, and so forth) simply by applying more resources to the problem. Therefore, they have a greater need to leverage the improvements mentors can help bring about—in skill sets, communication and cohesion, data sharing, and focus—if they want to improve software development performance overall.

This article addresses the basic requirements for growing "mentor capital" and providing a sound foundation for an organization's future. It explores the fundamentals of mentoring, discusses the benefits, and suggests criteria for good mentors.

BUILDING A MENTORING ENVIRONMENT

To understand what sort of environment is required for effective mentoring, think for a moment about the world of sports. Can you recall a single instance in which a coach refused to advise his team during a game? Refused to hold a practice? Neglected to give timely and honest feedback to his players? (Just think Woody Hayes of Ohio State!) I certainly can't. In that world, coaches know that the team members can't deliver what is expected unless the coach, as the leader, helps them along by sharing knowledge, providing moral support, and paying attention to what motivates his players. In addition, coaches know that they need to build leaders within the team: players in the trenches who can motivate their peers to achieve.

So, what can we do to cultivate that kind of understanding and behavior in the business world, specifically within the world of software development?

There are several ways to implement a mentoring environment within your organization, and all must start at the top. If an organization's leaders don't value mentoring, then neither will the rest of the team members. Although we don't have an official mentoring program at Rational, our field guidelines and core values demand knowledge sharing and leadership development on the part of every manager throughout the organization. An environment like ours is a prerequisite for a more "official" program, too. There will be no guarantee of involvement or success unless you first create a corporate culture that makes people feel mentoring is the right thing to do. If your company already has core values that encourage mentoring, then a well-conceived program might strengthen good practices that are already in place and create a more effective mentoring environment.

To establish a mentoring program, start with the end in mind. Do you want to create an environment that grooms future managers or one that improves skills, confidence, and ability within people's current positions? In addition, keep in mind that personnel in sales, product development, and consulting have different needs, desires, skills, and career paths, so the program should be designed to fit specific career fields. Trying to impose a "one-size-fits-all" mentoring program on an entire organization typically dilutes the initiative's effectiveness and value. It's important to anticipate the needs of those who want to cross disciplines, such as engineers who want to be in sales, product managers who want to be field consultants, and so on. For engineers, for example, it would make sense to assign a mentor who works with salespeople rather than match them with another engineer.

One approach I use to strengthen mentoring activities in my organization is to include them as measurements of both individual and team performance. When I do my teams' annual performance review, I spend a good part of the time discussing what knowledge transfer, skills improvement, and general corporate citizenship activities took place during the review period. I find that if I do this consistently, then both leaders and team members begin to look at situations with an added dimension: how to help others be successful and reach their goals.

MENTORING FUNDAMENTALS

No matter what mentoring approach you decide to use, you'll want to keep a few fundamentals in mind. In general, good mentors do the following:

- Facilitate thinking instead of giving the answer. Good mentors make you think, form your own conclusions, and then execute. They see themselves as facilitators and drivers.
- Encourage teams to take risks. Mentors push teams to experiment with new approaches and to rely on their instincts and experience to move in new directions, as

opposed to always doing things the same way or relying too heavily on numbers to drive a decision.

- Allow themselves to be vulnerable. Leaders who don't put up a shield, one that protects them from making a mistake (or from simply revealing that they are human and don't know everything), make it easier for their teams to build trust up the chain of command.

- Make team members feel responsible for everyone's success. A goal of any mentoring program should be to make many people, not just the manager, feel responsible for every team member's individual success, as well as for team success overall. This will make a huge increase in the amount of support and the number of ideas at your disposal to improve performance. You'll also get better cohesion across the team.

Benefits of a Mentoring Environment

According to Noel Tichy, author of *The Leadership Engine*,[1] all effective leaders strive to create mentoring environments within their organizations and teach others. There are many obvious reasons why this is advantageous: it increases an organization's capability, helps get the work done more efficiently, and so forth. What about the reasons that aren't so intuitive, however? In truth, these provide just as much or more value. Let me offer the following list.

Promotes Creativity and Risk-Taking

In cultures in which trust is lacking, people go into "protective mode"; they grow risk-averse and act only to ensure self-preservation. In contrast, when people feel they can trust others to give them honest and sincere feedback for the right reasons (i.e., to benefit the company as opposed to forwarding a selfish, personal agenda), they are more willing to open up, take risks, and forge ahead. In a software development organization in which communication and information sharing is critical for success, being in an environment where territorial boundaries between and within teams are broken down can only improve performance and productivity. Development organizations that foster open communication through mentoring can enjoy the benefit of the whole team's collective brainpower and effort.

SMOOTHES OUT THE DIPS

Being part of a culture that promotes open communication and trust also helps teams have a better chance of weathering the tough times and accelerating through the good ones. Good mentoring can produce an organization that consists of people who are on the same page, are capable of making the right decisions without being micromanaged, and are able to execute both within a team and as individuals. This creates a powerful foundation for getting through rough spots and persevering. Although, ultimately, it takes much more than trust and communication to achieve goals, having this foundation for the team is a must.

In addition, when challenging situations require everyone's effort, it's better to have a team of problem solvers rather than a collection of order takers. Mentoring can help ensure that team members know how to leverage their collective brainpower and work together to solve problems. They'll be far more likely to succeed than a team made up of individuals who are unable to think innovatively and unwilling to take chances.

ATTRACTS THE RIGHT PEOPLE

Winners like to be with winners. If you create an environment with a high level of trust and a high sense of mission and purpose—and if you give people the opportunity not only to reap financial rewards but also to grow as individuals—then you will attract people who appreciate and respond to those opportunities. Typically, people who have a bad case of the "What have you done for me lately?" syndrome—people who are interested only in their own good and how much money they can make— are not attracted to mentoring environments that require a lot of give and take.

You'll also be able to attract good people because a trusting and mentoring environment provides an infrastructure that can help all team members succeed. If a prospective employee knows that your software organization takes on entry-level personnel or people with skills that need to be developed, and that the entire team is invested in their success (and ultimately the team's success) and development, then he or she will feel totally confident about joining you. At the same time, new team members will know that they won't be able to "just get by," and that they must pull their own weight in helping to achieve the team's goals. Mentoring environments usually attract high performers to whom results and professional development are important.

People who believe in the corporate mission and like to work collaboratively are the people who help companies sustain performance through good times and bad. That brings me to my next point.

ENSURES LONG-TERM SURVIVAL

In *Good to Great*,[2] Jim Collins says that companies which have charismatic leaders do very well while that leader is running the show but begin to stumble after the leader goes. The reason? Charismatic leaders often force their people to do what the leader believes is right, instead of what is actually right for the company. In other words, people focus on making the leader happy even if it means doing the wrong thing for the company. In addition, Collins found, charismatic leaders make very poor mentors; they are wrapped up in their own worlds and have little interest in those around them.

Here's an interesting hypothetical question for all you managers out there: if your organization continues to execute very well while you are away on vacation, do you feel *sad* that they could do without you or *proud* that they could do without you? Likewise, if they stumble when you go on vacation, do you stick out your chest and proclaim, "They can't do it without me"?

If you fall into the camp of feeling sad when your team succeeds without you or comforted when it doesn't, that's a sign of trouble. Chances are there is not enough mentoring going on within your organization and people are depending on you to make all the decisions. Ultimately, if you do not groom new leaders, then the failures will increase—and you will look bad, too.

Remember, good managers teach their teams how to fish instead of just giving them the fish.

WHO SHOULD MENTOR?

Mentors don't have to be managers. I remember reading a case study for a management course years ago that focused on discovering who the real "influencers" were in an office. Over a period of several months, the researchers tracked how many visits each person in the office received from coworkers during the day and plotted the results on the office seating plan blueprint. Without seeing this blueprint, you might assume that managers received the most visits over time, but this was not the case. Non-managers received far more visits than managers. This study found the centers of power and influence in an organization do not necessarily reside within the management structure. When people come seeking advice and wisdom, it doesn't matter where you sit, how much money you make, or how fancy your title is. What matters most is a willingness to listen, give advice, provide feedback, and take genuine interest in a coworker's situation.

These qualities are key, whether your organization has a formal mentoring program or not. If the environment encourages it, then more people will work on developing good mentoring skills.

Generally, effective mentors do the following:

SHARE A TEACHABLE POINT OF VIEW.

Not all great athletes make great coaches, and the same can be said about knowledgeable, experienced employees *vis à vis* mentoring. Of course, it's important for mentors to have a broad spectrum of experience and interests so they can advise on multiple areas and topics. What really makes an effective mentor is the ability to translate those experiences into a form that is useful to others. That means being able to truly understand the core issues involved in another person's work so you can shape your lessons to address those issues. It also requires the ability to analyze that person's strengths and weaknesses so you can support the former and help him or her overcome the latter. In the cases of software development organizations, it helps if the mentor has been involved in failed, as well as successful, projects in several capacities (such as project manager, lead developer, or analyst, for example). It is also a benefit if the mentor has worked on various types of projects with different kinds of drivers and constraints. All of this variety leads to a well-rounded body of knowledge and experience one can draw from.

PROVIDE HONEST AND DIRECT FEEDBACK.

Some people avoid giving honest feedback because they want to avoid confrontation. To be of any help, however, a mentor must be able to tell people what they're doing wrong and provide constructive suggestions about how to correct it. Typically, this is a skill that people acquire over time, but some people never really become adept at it. If you plan to mentor, it helps to remember all the reasons why this type of feedback is important—it is to help someone see things in a different light and improve, and ultimately to contribute to the good of the organization.

EXERCISE PATIENCE AND DISCRETION.

The last thing anyone wants or needs when they're in a tough situation is to have someone broadcasting their issues throughout the organization. For trust to exist, discretion must be present too. Mentors need to make sure they keep things to themselves and do not violate the trust of the people they are advising. Being patient is also a key requirement when you take on the task of helping others. That includes allowing others to discover the answers, instead of just blurting the answers out yourself. The discovery process is key both to learning and to developing the motivation for taking corrective action.

UNDERSTAND THE ORGANIZATION AND HOW TO NAVIGATE IT.

Any situation involving a number of people includes dynamics that need to be understood and appreciated: Where does the power reside in the organization? What is driving the customer? Where are the icebergs and landmines? Why is a certain tool being chosen over another? Mentors should be able to play an important role in helping teams navigate through organizational issues, especially in software development, where lots of time, money, and resources are usually being consumed in order to deliver a system. It takes a wise and experienced person to recognize that people and organizations are not always driven by the obvious demands of quality, schedule, and so forth; instead, they might be trying to comply with secondary factors, such as company culture, fear of change or failure, or risk mitigation.

ARE YOU A CANDIDATE FOR MENTORING?

Just as it takes a certain kind of person to mentor, not everyone is a prime candidate for *being* mentored. When you link up with a coach, you must be willing to open yourself up to constructive feedback; you must be ready to face reality and attack the hard stuff. On the plus side, this can lead to achieving your goals and making remarkable improvements.

Of course, the first step in this process is recognizing that you need help or guidance. A few years ago, I hired a personal coach to help me smooth out a few of my "rough" spots—to help me listen better, communicate more effectively, and cultivate patience, as well as address a few other areas that needed attention. To do this, I had to take a hard look at myself and analyze where I most needed help. Then, I had to be willing to listen to sometimes painful feedback. "You're impatient," or, "You talk too much"; that's what I heard from my coach at first. Realizing that this process was going to make me a better person kept me focused and determined to go through with it.

My process began with giving concrete examples of the issues, why I felt they were a problem, and what I wanted the end result to be. Then, I formed my own solutions. As I noted above, mentors and coaches are there to guide and assess instead of just giving you the answers. Coming up with a solution is part of the learning process and makes the whole exercise worthwhile. In the end, if you come up with the solutions, and those solutions work, then you will value and appreciate the lessons you learn that much more.

Of course, in the workplace, not all mentoring gets down to such a personal level, but listening to criticism of your work can be just as painful. To get the most out of mentoring, I have found, you have to be willing to attack the toughest areas first. After that, the rest is much easier. Opening up and letting someone you trust dig, pry, or inject a dose of reality into your world is very liberating. If your mentor is doing it for the right reasons, it can make a critical difference to your career.

Once you're certain that you're ready for a mentor, finding an appropriate person is not always easy or obvious. It helps if you know what you need from a mentoring program. Do you want to develop technical skills or people skills? Do you need to get help with "reading" the organization or managing people? Knowing where you want to focus will help narrow your search and identify the type of mentor you are looking for.

SOUND INVESTMENT, HIGH RETURNS

Mentoring capital is just as important to an organization as its cash reserves are. If you invest carefully in creating a strong mentoring environment, then the returns can be very high for mentors, for those they advise, and, especially, for the organization as a whole. As Jim Collins points out in *Good to Great*, leaders who are ambitious for their company rather than for themselves seek to develop *other* leaders who can help drive the company in the right direction. Through mentoring, they build leaders for generations to come, people who can sustain the company's success over many years. In the context of a software development organization, passing on wisdom and best practices to develop leadership capability translates to continuous productivity, higher project success rates, and winning the confidence and support of the company's non-technical managers.

Do you feel your organization would improve with the help of a mentoring program? If you begin exploring the possibility of mentorship, then you will soon find others who want to participate and your organization can start realizing substantial benefits very quickly. A sound mentoring program can bring about improvements in capability, performance, communication, and team dynamics. It can also help those who mentor by teaching them how to lead more effectively, giving them a chance to make a positive contribution to the organization's overall good.

Notes

[1] Tichy, Noel M. *The Leadership Engine: How Winning Companies Build Leaders at Every Level*. Harper Business, 1997.

[2] Collins, Jim. *Good to Great: Why Some Companies Make the Leap... and Others Don't*. Harper Collins, 2001.

Appendix B: What I've Learned

1. **It is a privilege and an honor to manage people.** The decisions you make and the actions you take impact people's lives and their families' lives. Do not take this lightly or make uninformed decisions.

2. **Love and take care of your family and friends.** They depend on you more than you can imagine. Letting them down is a non-recoverable failure.

3. **You can only lead from the front, not the back.** If you are in a leadership position, be aware that what you say and do has a significant effect on the people who work for you. Lead by example, make the hard decisions, and live or die by your actions.

4. **Play with the uniform you were issued.** Don't be someone you're not or forget where you came from. Your roots are important to who you are, to your value system, and to what drives you.

5. **Honesty, trust, and integrity are overused words, but underused qualities.** You can never go wrong by having too much of these non-negotiable traits. You must demonstrate these every day.

6. **Don't undervalue people.** People skills are just as important as brains. How you treat and value people is a reflection of who you really are. There is enough success for everyone, so try to help people achieve the most out of life.

7. **You're only as good as your last record.** Don't live your life displaying perpetual arrogance because you once did something or lucked into something great. You have to deliver every day.

8. **Never confuse activity with results.** Make things happen and deliver. There are no substitutes for results.

9. **Intellectual curiosity will take you far.** Never stop learning and trying new things. There is no steady state when it comes to your development—you are either going forwards or backwards.

10. **Never forget those who helped you get where you are.** No one makes it alone, but how soon we forget that our climb up the ladder often occurs on the backs and hard work of others. Be thankful and gracious, and pay it forward.

11. **As you move up the ladder, remember the hard work is just beginning.** Never take the "I've arrived" approach. It's arrogant, shows shallowness, and demonstrates that you have no idea what your position or responsibilities are really about.

12. **Success and failure happen.** A fulfilled life is one that has a healthy dose of successes and failures. A very fulfilled life is one in which you learned more from your failures than your successes.

13. **When you need a relationship, it's too late to build one.** *(Credit for this goes to Dr. Lois Frankel).* The network is powerful and is one of the most valued assets in life. Meet as many people as you can and invest in relationships. You will be amazed at the outcomes.

14. **Don't criticize things you don't understand or those who take chances.** Unless you're in the game and on the field grinding it out every day, don't judge from the sidelines. Signing paychecks on the back is very different and requires much less responsibility than signing them on the front does.

15. **Karma is real.** What goes around comes around. It may not come when you want it to or in the form you desire, but, trust me, it does come. When you realize this, retaliation is no longer part of your DNA.

16. **If you have to say it, it ain't so.** Self-promotion embarrasses those who do it. If you are a true success, people will know. You don't have to tell them.

17. **Do you have twenty years of experience, or one year of experience twenty times?** Make choices that give you more choices and avoid playing it safe. Get out there and take some risks. Change things up, and broaden your horizons. You'll never go wrong with this approach.

18. **Are people your friends because of what you can do for them, or because of who you are?** Avoid those people with the "What have you done for me lately?" syndrome. You can tell who they are if they don't keep in contact with you after you can no longer help them.

19. **To have a positive attitude, avoid negative people.** Those around you will drive and influence your outlook, so stick with people who are upbeat and see the positive side of things.

20. **In the end, the love you take is equal to the love you make.** I have to give the Beatles credit for this one, but it is true that what you put into life is what you get out of it. There are no long-term shortcuts in life. You have to earn everything.

SIDNEY E. FUCHS

Sidney E. Fuchs is the President and Chief Executive Officer of MacAulay Brown, Inc. (MacB), a premier engineering and technical services company with over 2,000 employees worldwide. He is a leading executive with more than 25 years experience in Intelligence, National Security, Aerospace and Defense.

Prior to MacB, he was the CEO and a director of ATS Corporation (NYSE Amex: ATSC) and was the president and CEO and a director of OAO Technology Solutions (OAOT).

Prior to OAOT, Mr. Fuchs was a corporate vice president and officer of Northrop Grumman Corporation (NYSE: NOC), a Fortune 100® Aerospace and Defense company with over $30B in annual revenue where he held the position of president and CEO of TASC, Inc., a $1.2B subsidiary providing engineering expertise to the Intelligence, Aerospace, and Defense markets. Prior to Northrop Grumman, Mr. Fuchs held senior positions with Digital Equipment Corporation, Oracle Corporation, and Rational Software Corporation.

Mr. Fuchs is a former Central Intelligence Agency Officer having served in a number of operations and management positions. He has received several commendations from the Director of Central Intelligence and the US Defense and Intelligence Community.

In 2012, he was inducted into the Louisiana State University College of Engineering Hall of Distinction and has received federal appointments to the National Defense University Board of Visitors and the Defense Science Board.

Mr. Fuchs is the Chairman of the Board of Governors of the Tower Club Tyson's Corner and the Chairman of the LSU Department of Mechanical Engineering Industrial Advisory Board. He has served on the boards of several public and private corporations and has been an advisor to various companies and private equity firms.

He earned BS and MS degrees in Mechanical Engineering from Louisiana State University and has completed executive programs at the University of Virginia Darden School, the University of Pennsylvania Wharton School, Harvard University, and the University of Chicago Graduate School of Business.

A recognized thought leader, Mr. Fuchs is an internationally published author and speaker on leadership, organizational change, business strategy and operations, and National Security.

FACEBOOK:

https://www.facebook.com/GetOffTheBench

TWITTER:

https://twitter.com/#!/GetOfftheBench

LINKEDIN:

http://www.linkedin.com/groups/Get-Off-Bench-Unleashing-Power-4394120?home=&gid=4394120&trk=anet_ug_hm

WEBSITE:

www.sidfuchs.com

EMAIL:

sid@sidfuchs.com

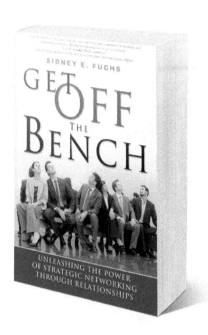

How can you use this book?

MOTIVATE

EDUCATE

THANK

INSPIRE

PROMOTE

CONNECT

Why have a custom version of *Get Off The Bench*?

- Build personal bonds with customers, prospects, employees, donors, and key constituencies
- Develop a long-lasting reminder of your event, milestone, or celebration
- Provide a keepsake that inspires change in behavior and change in lives
- Deliver the ultimate "thank you" gift that remains on coffee tables and bookshelves
- Generate the "wow" factor

Books are thoughtful gifts that provide a genuine sentiment that other promotional items cannot express. They promote employee discussions and interaction, reinforce an event's meaning or location, and they make a lasting impression. Use your book to say "Thank You" and show people that you care.